CONTENTS

THE VENEZUELA CASE

An story to how 21st Century Socialism destroyed a country.

By: Fernando Germán M.

To my country ... that saw me born and grow, and that
today, despite being far away, I do not forget.

Explanatory note: The name of the author Fernando Guzmán M, is
fictitious. This is so, for security reasons, since the rights and security
of the authentic author, and his family, can be violated by the Chavista
regime.

It is my first publication in English. If they detect a flaw in the writing, I
apologize. I hope, that to some extent, you can understand the message
of my book.

FROM MODERN VENEZUELA TO BACKWARD VENEZUELA

More than 20 years ago, I left my beloved Venezuela, and escaped to Spain, fleeing the eminent danger that lurked in the country at that time: The Bolivarian Revolution.

In my long exile, in the so-called "mother country", when someone found out that I was from Venezuela, and they asked me about what happened in my country, after telling some facts, and seeing that the person, or people, were left with a face of astonishment, later I told them, that with everything I've seen, and lived, if someday I write a book about what was happening in Venezuela, possibly the people who read it, would come to the conclusion, that everything described in that book, it is a lie, or a brutal exaggeration.

An example of this was what happened on August 4, 2018, when there was a "supposed" attack against Venezuelan "president" Nicolás Maduro, with some drones, during the celebration of an event in Caracas. A person of Spanish origin who knew me, told me that what happened in Caracas with the attack, to him, seemed "a Chinese story", and gave him the impression that "everything had been a show set by Maduro", to which I replied that, like him, there are millions of other people around the world who think the same. The sad thing of the story, is that in my Venezuela, there are still people, who believe blindly, the version that the Chavista government gives of this fact. And worse, for more than twenty years, there are people who have gone believing, all the stories of the regime, despite having increased brutally hunger and misery in the country in all that time, and all in the name of the call " socialism of the 21st century ".

On occasion, I have met Spaniards, who have lived in the Venezuela of the 60s and 70s, and all of them agree, who do not understand, how the country has had a brutal change of wealth, to extreme poverty.

During the boom in oil prices, especially in the 70s, the country was given billions of dollars, and it could be said that it was a kind of Saudi Venezuela. I still remember that many Venezuelans, on weekends, were traveling by plane to Miami, Florida, in the United States (USA) to buy everything, and they were spending a lot of money. Many defined that generation as "the cheap Ta! Give me two! " The problem is that during the first government of Carlos Andrés Pérez (1974 -1979), a culture of waste was created. Such culture has penetrated, that today, despite the chaos, there are still people who have not changed that way of thinking, especially in the Chavista people who are in the highest spheres of power, who still believe, who still live in the Saudi Venezuela.

I still remember that phrase of the writer, and Venezuelan intellectual, Doctor Arturo Uslar Pietri, who said that "We must sow Petroleum". This phrase comes from an article that wrote Uslar Pietri in a newspaper in 1932, and that despite having passed more than 80 years, that phrase even today is valid, since no government since then, has managed to manage that great wealth: the so-called black gold.

In the 70s, unfortunately, the government did not know how to take advantage of this great economic boom, and the contradictory thing is that despite the fact that billions of dollars were coming in, on the other hand, the government began borrowing money from the Monetary Fund International (IMF), and various foreign banks. In short, it is impossible to believe that a country full of money, which could lend money to the same IMF, rather, did the opposite. Possibly, the vision of the government of that time, was to enjoy, and to waste, without having a slight idea that if one day the price of Petroleum (oil) fell, it could have its consequences. And the 80s came, and the consequences. The price of Petroleum fell, and Venezuela, was in an extreme situation, that had an unpayable external debt. And from there, the country began little by little, to decay.

Between 1973 and 1984, 145 billion dollars came into the country thanks to Petroleum. That burrada of money, is equivalent to 10 times the money used with the famous Marshall Plan, which was used to rebuild all of Europe after the Second World War.

A, but most incredible of all this history, is that during the 20 years of Chavism, the country received more than 775 billion dollars, and today, to give an example, in hospitals, there are no medicines, or most basic elements, to attend to a patient.
Throughout the book, I will comment on some cases, which could explain, where all that money was going to end up. In short, I could tell you that thanks to the so-called "Bolivarian revolution", in Venezuela it was accentuated in a brutal and aberrant way, waste, corruption, protectionism, populism, ease, rentism, and above all , the negligence. With all these elements, one can clearly understand why Venezuela today is as it is.

I was born in what was once the most modern motherhood in Latin America, located in the city of Caracas, the maternity Concepción Palacios. For the year 2019, interestingly, it is the worst maternity in Latin America, thanks to the lack of maintenance and supplies. There are those who affirm that such motherhood has the highest mortality rate of unborn in the world! Such is gloomy reality, that the same Chavista government, for years refuses to provide figures or statistics of deaths in health centers. And it does not give figures on violent deaths in the streets, or in prison centers.

In my first years of life, Venezuela, gave me the opportunity to train as a good citizen. I studied both in public and private schools. My parents had worked hard to give my brothers and me the best education. In Venezuela, both at the level of public and private institutes, there were good infrastructures and highly qualified personnel.

When I was about 11 years old, an aunt on the maternal side, I had taken, out of curiosity, to a rally of a political party called COPEI (Independent Electoral Political Committee), which was of Christian Democratic ideology. Being a child, and unknowingly, I had started to like politics, and with 12 years, I had joined to the youth organization of that party, which was known as the Copeyana Revolutionary Youth (JRC). To participate in the JRC, one of the requirements was to be at least 14 years old. But, in my case, seeing my interest, they made an exception.

By December of 1978, presidential elections were going to take place, and at that time, with my 12 years, I had already attended several electoral campaign events of the party. The candidate of my party at that time, was Doctor Luis Herrera Campins. From one of those meetings, I had brought a souvenir, which consisted of a huge poster or poster, with the candidate's photo. Said souvenir, I had kept it well folded inside one of my notebooks that I used to go to classes in my school. At that time, I was studying the last year of primary education. The last day of classes, before the presidential elections, being with my classmates in my classroom, one of my friends, I had borrowed one of my notebooks to take some notes, and I had forgotten, that inside that notebook I had kept my poster with the candidate's photo. My partner, saw the folded sign, and unfolded it inside the classroom. My teacher, who was in favor of another presidential candidate, when he saw the poster displayed, which was more than a meter high, my teacher gave a shout scream, asking who of was that poster, and immediately some of my colleagues did not hesitate point to me Immediately my teacher took me from one of my arms, and almost dragged me, she took me to the principal's office, demanding the director, that they should expel me for a few days. The director called my mother, who was at the door of the school, since she was going to pick me up every day to take me home, and the director tells her what happened, and tells her, that I have saved from an expulsion, because that was the last day of activity before the holidays.

Luis Herrera Campins.

For the next elections in 1983, I already worked as a member in the Organization Secretariat of the JRC, and I lived a very active electoral campaign, carrying out activities to register new members in the party. We were a group of about 10 young people, who attended the most important rallies, to register people who attended these events. That year, my candidate was Dr. Rafael Caldera, who was a prominent leader, founder of the party, and president of Venezuela in the late 60s. Unfortunately, in these elections of '83, won the main opposition party, called Action Democratic (AD). So we had as president, Jaime Lusinchi, popularly known in the underworld, as "Borrachinchi", since he was engaged in drinking a lot of alcohol.

For the following elections of 1988, I continued to actively participate in the JRC, as well as in the electoral campaign, supporting the candidate of my party, which was at that time, Eduardo Fernández. On this occasion, the elections were won again by AD, with Carlos Andrés Pérez.

Carlos Andrés Pérez.

After taking office as president in early 1989, Carlos Andrés decided to raise the price of gasoline, which led to a social outbreak, which came to be called "the Caracazo", where thousands of people, throughout the In this country, they sacked stores, and the security forces (police, army and National Guard) took to the streets to violently repress looters and demonstrators.

The events took place between the 27th of February to the 8th of March. The official figures would report some 276 deaths, and thousands of wounded. Some unofficial reports spoke of more than 300 people deceased, and 2000 missing.

I had to live these violent events in the Venezuelan city of Valencia. I remember, that on the television, they transmitted images of people looting stores, and supermarkets.

The causes of this social outbreak, has its origin in the economic policies of the previous governments of Luis Herrera, and especially, Jaime Lusinchi, who indebted the country more, creating a real economic crisis, with inflation and devaluation of the currency , which led the elected president Carlos Andrés, to the application of a package of economic measures, popularly known as "the paquetazo", which resulted in a social outbreak of hatred and violence, which had never been lived in the country. These causes, later, Hugo Chávez, would use them to justify his two military coups attempts.

THE FIRST MILITARY COUP AT-
TEMPT OF THE 4F

The first attempt of military uprising occurred on February 4 (4F), when President Pérez returned by plane from the World Economic Forum in Davos, in Switzerland. Thanks to the opportune performance of the personnel that accompanied him, especially of the members of the Presidential Civil Guard, Pérez was able to take refuge successfully in the presidential palace of Miraflores in Caracas. Thanks to some of his escorts, Perez later manages to reach the television station Venevisión, from where he informed to the country on two occasions to report on the situation.

The assault on the presidential palace by the military coup leaders began at 12 midnight in 4F. At the same time military rebels under the command of Miguel Rodríguez Torres, assaulted the presidential residence (La Casona) in Caracas. Meanwhile, in other important cities of the country, the confrontations between loyal and military coup forces were intense, in some cases.

Failed the capture of the city of Caracas, the insurgents surrendered in the capital, and the leader, Hugo Chávez, was arrested in Caracas. Despite being detained the leader of the uprising, in some barracks, his followers in the military coup plot, were still fighting. So the government, sought a way to convince those who remained rebels, to lay down their weapons. The decision was to opt for the leader of the attempted military coup, appear before the television cameras, so that he himself Chávez, call his colleagues to hand over the weapons and surrender

During his short speech before the cameras, Chávez pronounced a phrase that would be recorded in the minds of all those who heard his words, the famous "for now".

That same day, many people understood that in that phrase "for now", Chávez announced that he would try again. The question is that almost nobody knew how and when. In my land, there is a popular saying that says: "When the river sounds ... stones bring". It is a way of saying, that there is something in the environment about to burst, such as another military coup d'état.

Chávez calls on his fellow rebels to lay down their arms.

After the surrender of the rebels, some 200 officers, including Chávez, were tried for military rebellion in 1992, and sentenced to prison. In 1994, all the military coup leaders, would be released after a so-called "pardon".

Of the 32 people who died during the attempted military coup, today, many of their families still await justice.

THE SECOND MILITARY COUP ATTEMPT OF 27N

On November 27, 1992 (27N), a group of militarys, with the help of ultra left activists belonging to the Red Flag, and third road, carry out an attempted military coup d'état. Its main objective was to capture President Pérez, and establish a civic-military junta. Among the military, the Inspector General of the Navy Hernán Grüber Odremán stands out as supposed head, supported by Vice Admiral Luis Enrique Cabrera Aguirre, Lieutenant Colonel of aviation Luis Reyes Reyes, and Brigadier General (Aviation) Francisco Visconti Osorio.

Unlike the previous attempted military coup of 4F, on this occasion, the rebels if they were worried about taking the the television channels stations and some radio stations. In the case of the national television station Venezolana de Televisión (VTV), the idea of the military coup plotters was to occupy their facilities as they were, and to transmit a video with a message from the military coup leaders. The issue is that in its place, another video was recorded previously recorded with a message from Chávez, who, supposedly, had not participated in the planning of the military coup, to the surprise of the ringleaders. I imagine the face they put, when the conspirators saw Chávez on television, instead of the recorded message of the military coup leaders.

The subject of the video, to some extent, is not very clear, if within the same group of military coup plotters, a group conspired to promote the image of Chavez, as the supposed leader of the second attempt. If we take into account, that the original idea of the military coup plotters was to broadcast a video with a message from the leaders, well, within the group, someone planned in advance to put in its place, another video with a

12

message from Chavez, with the idea , to imply, that a man who was in prison, participated in the planning of a second military coup d'état. Moreover, recording a video in secret, inside a maximum security military prison, in the same cell where Chávez was, is not an easy thing. Someone in the highest levels of the army and the government had to give the facilities for it.

Returning to the events of 27N, while the military coup plotters tried to achieve their goals, Perez was able to reach a channel called Televen, which was not occupied by the rebels, and there, the president issued a message, announcing that everything was under control. That same day, the rebels who had taken VTV, surrendered, after a hard armed confrontation.

Image of the video with the message recorded by Chávez.

On the morning of that 27N day, OV-10 Bronco planes, piloted by military coup officers, took off from the Libertador Air Base in Maracay, near Caracas, and attacked several targets throughout the country, where the bombing of the Miraflores Palace stands out. and the Generalissimo Francisco de Miranda Air Base, in Caracas.

Around four o'clock in the afternoon, some of the ringleaders escaped from the country by plane to Peru, where they were received as political persecuted by President Alberto Fujimori.

The military coup plot culminated in the death of 171 people (142 civilians and 29 militarys).

Five hundred officers and NCOs were arrested following the doings, along with 800 rankless soldiers and 40 civilians. Of these, some 196 people, including civilians and soldiers, were taken to a military court. Of these, 97 were convicted, and the rest were acquitted. However, a few weeks later, the Supreme Court of Justice (SCJ) annulled the trials. In the end, all those involved were released by the governments of Ramón J. Velásquez and Rafael Caldera.

Three days after the events of 27N, I was able to see in person one of the walls of the Miraflores palace, which had been hit by a bomb that exploded, knocking down part of the wall. Near there, on the Carmelite bridge, I saw on the ground, the mark of a bomb impact launched by one of the planes manned by the military coup plotters, which had not exploded. I remember, one of the many things that were commented in those days, was that many of the bombs dropped by the OV-10 Bronco planes did not explode, and that if you had fulfilled their function, surely there would have been talk of a greater tragedy with hundreds of dead.

In relation to the case of the famous video that was not conveyed with the message of the military coup leaders, much speculation was raised by those who had participated in the planning of the supposed video. What is known is that there were two videos, and that someone conspired within the group of military coup, to transmit the video with the message of

Chavez.

More than 20 years after the events, I think, it is still unknown exactly who were the real intellectual authors of the second coup attempt. And if in case they had managed to overthrow the Perez government, or if they had succeeded, It is also unknown who who would be the members of that supposed military civic junta announced in the two videos One thing if I have clear. The head of said civic military junta would be Chávez. In fact, many of the military coup leaders, later, had stated that one of the objectives was to free Chávez from jail. What they do not say, was with what end, or who was he who gave the order to record the video with the message of Chavez.

Another issue to be taken into account is that the video that came to be transmitted with the message of Chávez was made a few hours before the military coup, when he was imprisoned in a maximum security military prison. That is to say, he was recorded the video in his dungeon, with his camouflage uniform and red beret, announcing on behalf of the Bolivarian Revolutionary Movement 200 (MRB 200), that a new Bolivarian revolution was taking place, and "that at that very moment", they had went out into the streets to fight, suggesting that the Perez government had already fallen, and that the military coup leaders had already assumed power, announcing that a new government formed by what he called a "Bolivarian Patriotic Junta", and he had assumed control of the country. In short, the authors of the video, had the premeditated intention, to try to strain a recorded video, as a live broadcast and direct, to convey to viewers, that there was a new government.

On the other hand, the military coup leaders who had taken VTV, broadcast live and direct, a few short messages in the name of the 5th of July Movement, where the population was called to take to the streets to join the military coup, and that the loyal military to the Perez government, they would surrender, or else they would be victims of bombing. The question is that those who assumed the task of issuing the messages, in my opinion, did not give the slightest confidence. The first one who spoke giving his revolutionary message, on the table, had placed a weapon, and on it, his trembling right hand, which seemed to have an attack of epilepsy or anxiety.

As for the take or occupation by the VTV military coup plotters, it was bloody, as there were 19 deaths. After the events, it was announced the case of two unarmed vigilantes, whom the military conspirators, they executed with a shot. The golpistas entered the television channel destroying everything with bursts of gunfire, not caring if they killed innocents on their way. They tried to close the street to avoid the possible arrival of forces loyal to the government, for which, in the middle of public thoroughfare, they shot the vehicles that were circulating there killing their occupants, with the only idea, to use those vehicles as obstacles in the Street. Within the VTV channel, they threatened to kill the few employees who were there, if they did not help in their mission to transmit their messages calling the population to join the "revolution". And everything under the command of Lieutenant Jesse Chacón. After the arrival of loyal forces to the government, and a strong confrontation, in the end, Chacón surrendered along with the military coup plotters.

The issue is that Chacón was sentenced to 22 years in prison, and later with Caldera's "pardon" in 1999, he was released. After the arrival of Chávez to power, he held important positions within the government, being one of them, the General Director of the National Telecommunications Commission (CONATEL) in 2001, the body that managed and regulated telecommunications in the country. Being director, I create the famous "gag law", and fixed its strategy to persecute the media. That is, we have a person who commanded the armed take, violent, with dead and wounded, of a television channel in 1992, and 10 years later, Chávez designated him as the highest authority to monitor and punish the media. A, subsequently, in 2003, he was appointed Minister of Communications, in 2004 he was Minister of Interior, in 2007 Minister of Telecommunications and Information Technology, in 2009 Minister for Science, Technology and Intermediate Industries, in 2013 Minister of Electric Energy, and in 2017, Maduro appointed him as ambassador of Venezuela in Austria. And all this has been achieved, thanks to the fact that in 1992, he commanded the armed and violent takeover of a television channel, with the resulting in 19 deaths.

As for who was the real organizing leader of the second military attempt, I think, it was Chavez himself. I insist ... the fact of having recorded a video announcing a new revolutionary government, it gives him away. With this, it is perfectly understood, that he was part of the organization of the second military coup from jail, with which, he knew perfectly who were part of the plot, its organization and purposes. Remember that phrase "for now" that pronounced the 4F ?. I think, long before the 4F, I had already planned the two military attempts. That is, they had already established, that if one failed, they had another second option up their sleeve. It is noteworthy that between the two military attempts, there was a period of six months, and believe me, planning a second military coup d'état, where there was a high level of participation and organization, is not done in six months. Moreover, there are some of the military coup leaders, who have indicated that their initial intention was to do it a month before.

What I do not understand about the government of Carlos Andrés, is that after surviving two military coups d'état, and having in his hands evidence that Chávez had participated actively from prison, Pérez did nothing, to avoid, that Hugo Chávez, continue to conspire from the prison. Moreover, after 27N, Chavez was allowed to continue his normal life inside the prison, with visits from friends and supporters, and of course, they let him continue planning his strategy to come to power.

Fernando Germán M

In short, the time he was held, possibly, helped him to understand that he had already failed two military coup attempts, and that a third unsuccessful attempt could have serious consequences. So, he decided use the same strategy that Adolf Hitler used in 1930 to get to power: to use the "democratic" way of elections.

And what was the fate of the supposed chief ringleaders of the 27N military coup attempt?. After being pardoneds in 1999:

Hernán Grüber Odremán, in 1998 he ran as a candidate for a governorship of the country. After losing, Chavez, as a consolation prize, appointed him in 1999 as Governor of the Federal District (Caracas), and after various accusations of corruption, he left political life.

To Luis Enrique Cabrera Aguirre, Chávez reinstates him to the military life in 1999, and in 2012, he becomes famous, since there are denunciations where he is linked to drug trafficking activities.

Luis Reyes Reyes, in 1999, the "commander" appointed him as Minister of infrastructure areas, and between 2002 and 2008, he is governor of Lara state. After leaving the government, Chávez appoints him as Minister of Popular Power for the Secretariat of the Presidency.

And in the case of Francisco Visconti Osorio, in 1998 he joins Chávez's party, and is elected as a member of the National Constituent Assembly of 1999. In 2018, he is launched as a presidential candidate to compete against Maduro. Visconti is supported by the Frente Amplio Nacional Bolivariano, a group of anti-Maduro chavistas. In the end, his candidacy was not accepted by the electoral authorities, since these authorities are ends in the interests of Maduro.

And as for the rest of the participants in the two military attempts, well, I could say that for the vast majority of the military coup leaders have made much use of the excuse of the "revolution"after the arrival of the "commander" to power. But, I think, with the examples I have given, such as the case of Jesse Chacón, you can make an idea, which has been the criterion of the Chavez government, to select those who would be part of the highest spheres of decision making in the country.

Well ... I think, I should comment on a separate special case. The of Diosdado Cabello, who in 2018, served as President of the National Constituent Assembly. And how did he get to that important position? It all started the 4F, when being a lieutenant, and he participated with Chávez in the attempted military coup. After supporting his "commander" in the 1998 elections, in 2001, the "commander" named him Vice President of the Republic. In 2002, he temporarily took the presidency of the country for a few hours, while Chávez had suffered what I would call a State military coup. In 2002 he assumed the Ministry of Justice. In 2004 he won elections for governor of the Miranda state, thanks to the institutional and financial support of the Chavez government. In 2008, after losing regional elections, Chávez gives him as a consolation prize, the portfolio of Minister of Public Works. In 2010 he was elected deputy, and then in 2012, appointed as president of the National Assembly with a Chavista majority. After the victory of the opposition in the next parliamentary elections, Maduro creates his version of parallel parliament 100% chavista (National Constituent Assembly), and is appointed to finger by Maduro as president of that Assembly. And all these high positions are achieved thanks to the fact that in 1992, he participated a military coup took place alongside Chávez. As an anecdote, the woman of Cabello, Marleny Contreras, in 2015 she was Minister of Tourism, and in 2018, Minister of Public Works. And what was the merit to get those charges? Well, the simple fact of being the wife of someone who participated in the military coup d'état of 1992.

And so, during more than 20 years of chavismo, high-rank-

Fernando Germán M

ing government officials, ministries, strategic state companies, judges, prosecutors, and everything that represents power, has been occupied by people like Jesse Chacón, or Diosdado Cabello. People, that his only professional merit, is to have participated and supported a military coup d'etat next to Chávez. And without forgetting, that this same "Chavez lineage", placed to family and friends in high positions to finger, occupying positions without these people have the slightest professional qualification for it.

THE RISE OF CHÁVEZ

After living two consecutive presidential electoral losses of my COPEI party, in 1993, an internal wing of the party, asked that Caldera was again the candidate, while another sector, wanted to repeat Eduardo Fernandez. After several internal disputes, COPEI decided to expel its founder from its ranks, with which, I saw, in my opinion, that a great injustice had been done.

After this expulsion, many sectors and political groups demanded that Caldera launch himself as a candidate, but he refused, insisting that without a new political party to support him, he would not launch into that electoral adventure. So a new party emerged, called National Convergence, which, along with other parties, formed a common front, and thanks to that, Caldera won the elections.

After taking office in February 1994, one of the things, which I consider, was Caldera's biggest mistake as President, was to give in to social pressure to process the release of Hugo Chávez.

Today in Venezuela, almost nobody remembers, the great current of opinion that existed in the environment on the idea of pardoning the military coup plotters. Claudio Fermín of AD, Oswaldo Álvarez Paz of COPEI, and Andrés Velásquez of Cause R, Caldera's main rivals in the presidential contest of 1993, had spoken publicly in favor of a general amnesty for all the military coup-makers of 1992, and they had committed themselves to set them free. It was the reflection of a predominant opinion in the country, and that focused directly on the media.

It is noteworthy that during that election campaign, the only candidate who did not speak out about a liberation of the military coup leaders was Caldera.

So, curiously, I won the elections, the only candidate who did not campaign announcing a pardon to Chavez. By the way, there are, who claim, that Caldera won, that's precisely why.

The problem is that after confirming the new government, Caldera surrounded himself with real inept people, people who sympathized with the idea of letting Chávez loose. Say they Chávez in the prison, it was more dangerous than being on the street.

Now, if Caldera had not moved a single finger to free Chávez, I am sure that Chávez would never have participated as a presidential candidate, since a person serving a sentence for military rebellion, under Venezuelan law, would not have been allowed be a presidential candidate.

On April 27, 92, the Minister of Defense, General Fernando Ochoa Antich, personally visited the detainees in the San Carlos Barracks, and according to the newspaper El Nacional, he "promised to plead for them to be released, as long as demonstrate sincere repentance for their actions against institutionality."

And there is even more ... On October 18, the governor of Zulia state, and subsequent presidential candidate by COPEI, Álvarez Paz, stated in the newspaper El Nacional, that "Claudio Fermín's statements regarding the possibility of decreeing a amnesty for the military and hooded were surprising and interesting, coming from a high representative of Acción Democrática "; and added: "Amnesty is necessary, because democracy wins." So, who would be the presidential candidates of AD and COPEI the following year, already expressed very clearly in favor of the liberation of the military coup plotters.

To this stream of pardon, is added, for example, the former president Luis Herrera Campíns de COPEI, with a statement to the press on November 2, 1992, where he said that "he considers it possible that the rebels of February can provide ideas to leave of the crisis, so he challenges President Pérez to release them and allow them to look for their votes in the street. "

Also the church, through the Archbishop of Caracas, Cardinal Lebrun Moratinos, had stated that "It was preferable to have the military coup plotters in the street looking for votes that conspiring and organizing rebellions in a prison."

And we must not forget the other great presidential candidate then, the radical Andrés Velásquez, of the R cause, who in his first act of electoral campaign in 1993, said that "If I win the elections, my first decrees will be to pardon everyone the officers prosecuted for attempted military coups d'etat. Pérez is the one who should be imprisoned, not them. " A detail to highlight, is that during the campaign of 1993, the Cause R sent as candidate to the Congress to one of the leaders of the military coup of 4-F, the commander Francisco Arias Cárdenas, still being detained, and that in the end it was not possible to register because they had not given him military discharge license.

I insist, it can not be denied, that public opinion, in a majority way, expressed its total agreement with the release of the military coup leaders of 4-F. And from that opinion were also spokespersons social media.

On the other hand, we must remember that before the so-called "pardon", the same Carlos Andrés, and his temporary successor in office, Ramón J. Velásquez, both, being Presidents active in their posts, had already granted freedom to numerous linked military to the two military attempts of 1992.

When Caldera assumed the presidency in 1998, and possibly against his will, he was forced to "pardon" the remaining militarys who were still awaiting trial. Surely within the head of Caldera, at the time of processing the freedom of the putschists, would say to himself, if it is what people want, he he washed his hands as did Pontius Pilate.

After spending two years in prison along with ten officers for leading the civil-military rebellion of 4F, on March 26, 1994, Hugo Chávez was released from the jail of San Francisco de Yare.

As it has been suggested, Chávez was granted a reprieve for dismissal of the case. On the other hand, there are those who swear that it was only a pardon. Others say that it was not a pardon, since in order to be granted, Chávez should have received a final sentence, something that did not happen with him. And finally, we find those who affirm that what Caldera granted was only a dismissal of the case, since according to the legislation of the moment, the president had the power to grant it.

Moments of the liberation of Chávez in 1994.

However, the dismissal of the case is the closing of a criminal investigation in process. But for this closure, it has to be argued that it is for lack of causes that justify the action of justice. And as far as I know, a person who organized two military coups, with dead bodies on their backs, is not exactly a lack of cause that justifies the action of justice. Now, in the face of this, there are those who allege, that it was done as a matter of national security.

Anyway, either way, Caldera was pressured, and forced to remove Chavez from prison, and curiously, today many accuse him for being the direct cause of the arrival of Chavez to power.

There is an anecdote that occurred one day with Caldera, who was visiting a clinic, and a nurse recriminated him that because of him, Chávez is President, to which the veteran politician answered the following:

"Miss, I'll be clear, brief and concise ... I did not vote for him. And you?"
After listening to Caldera's blunt response, the nurse disappeared from sight.

By the way, today there are thousands of Venezuelans like the happy nurse, who are still pointing their accusing finger at Caldera, and it turns out, that in their day, many of those accusers had voted blindly for the "commander".

Then, and in the end, whose fault is it that Chávez was president?.

MY SITUATION BEFORE AN UN-
CERTAIN FUTURE

I remember how more than one said "Venezuela a Cuba ?, you're crazy!" ... "nothing happens here", or I heard expressions like "that crazy man" was never going to win an presidential election.

I remember that in May of 1996, I went to the headquarters of the Ministry of Education in Caracas, to legalize my degrees, since I had considered, that in case of leaving the country, to continue my studies in journalism. The day I went to the Ministry, I had arrived around 10 o'clock in the morning, and they told me that they could not attend me, since only about 100 people attended each day, and already, at that time, the quota was completely full. And I asked how is that, and they answered me that if I wanted to be treated, I had to come one day at dawn to stand in line and sign up on a list. So the next day, I arrived at 4 in the morning, and there were already at that moment, in the queue, about 50 people listed on the list. So I signed up, and in the end, around 11 in the morning, I was able to deliver the documentation.

What I experienced that day at the Ministry of Education, showed me that there were many more people who thought the same way as me, who were planning to leave the country because of fear of an uncertain future. The question is that these people belonged to what I would call a silent minority, which quietly began to leave the country.

In those days, I also saw in the environment a kind of thirst for revenge on the part of a section of the population, disgusted with traditional parties. Many people wanted to see if the threats of the "commander" were fulfilled, to put all the corrupt politicians in prison, and to shoot a few. What those people did not see at that time, is that many of those "corrupt" left the old political parties, to be included in the new project of Chávez, with the idea of continuing to steal, but now, on behalf of the "revolution".

I did not understand Venezuelan society at the time. And no matter how much I explained to my friends, the vision I had of reality, but most of them considered me crazy. So, I chose to resign myself, since I saw clearly that a part of the Venezuelan people was thirsty for revenge, and that the "commander" would do his justice.

Since 1994, I had been thinking about my future for two years, if Chavismo came to power. And unfortunately, with the evolution of the events, I was forced to leave everything, and leave the country, in search of another more stable environment. So, I decided, against my will, to exile myself.

At the end of 1996, I left Caracas, to Europe, and decided to leave behind everything I wanted. After moving to Spain, I made the paperwork to finish the career of journalism in Madrid, and also legalized my academic degrees of Venezuela.

One thing that caused me a certain astonishment, after my arrival in Madrid, was the general opinion that the Spaniards of Venezuela had at that time, in 1996. For example, there were people who asked me what the end of a Venezuelan soap opera was, that back then, It was very famous on television channels in Spain. But if I asked more than one Spanish citizen about the impression they had on the situation in Venezuela, I met people who had a certain sympathy with the figure of Chavez, without knowing in broad strokes, the messages of his incendiary speeches. In fact, more than one, they saw him as him as a kind of reincarnation of Fidel Castro. So I decided to disconnect for a while to talk about politics of my country, and I dedicated myself to work and study.

CHÁVEZ'S FIRST VICTORY

In 1998 the Presidential race begins, and they are launched as candidates: Luis Alfaro Ucero for AD, Irene Sáez Conde (COPEI), Henrique Salas Romer (Project Venezuela), and Hugo Chávez Frías for the V Republic Movement (MVR).

In June 1998, several surveys were released, and at that time, the leader was Irene Sáez, and in the last place, with only 7%, Hugo Chávez.

For that moment, the diverse media of Venezuela, are dedicated to make an indirect campaign in favor of Hugo Chávez. It was impressive the open support given by businessman Gustavo Cisneros to the candidate, in all senses: Economic, media, including programming programs such as Los Peñonazos de Peña, led by journalist Alfredo Peña, and La Silla Caliente, from Oscar Yánez. They were joined by former director of Radio Caracas Televisión (RCTV) Marcel Granier, with his program Primer Plano, as well as Armas Camero, of the television channel Televen, with the program of José Vicente Rangel. All of them, I insist, helped to a great extent, to glorify the figure of Chávez. Many media entrepreneurs, such as Miguel Henrique Otero, of the newspaper El Nacional, devoted themselves to spreading in the covers of his diary, how much foolishness Chávez said, thus increasing an excessive publicity for his campaign.

To these media owners, he was joined by businessmen and academics, such as the Rector of the Simón Bolívar University, Ernesto Mayz Vallenilla, and other personalities, who with their direct or indirect support contributed to Chávez's coming to the Presidency of the country.

There is, who points as guilty Rafael Caldera of that Chavez is President, thanks to the "pardon". The question is, I believe, that there are more guilty parties, such as the media. The irony is that many of those guilty 20 years later, today they deny Chavez, and others, to some extent, are still kneeling before the regime.

Likewise, we must remember that the electoral campaign of the AD and COPEI parties was very bad, since they had withdrawn their candidates, to later support Salas Romer, which caused great annoyance in the militancy of both campaign commands and their followers, contributing thus, to put on a silver platter, the arrival to power of Chávez.

A curious detail of the Chavez campaign was the treatment of his image with some advisors, who sought to measure in detail, the letter and slogans of his speeches, including, his way of dressing. This, normally, usually happens with any presidential candidate, in any country. There are people who still believe, that the barbarities that loosed in their speeches, were improvised or proper to him. But nothing could be further from reality, when everything was planned in advance. A clear example of this planning in terms of its image, was its constant appearance with a military uniform campaigning. Interestingly, no one from the opposition hit the scream in the sky, or denounced before the competent authorities, that an ex-military who retired with dishonor, for planning two military coups, continued wearing the uniform as if he were still an active military man. Undoubtedly, that image of the "revolutionary" military man in his red beret, sought to create a kind of similarity with the famous image of "Che Guevara" wearing a beret. Finally, with Chávez, a personal brand image was created, with the sole purpose of getting followers and votes. However, if the competent military authorities at that time, and the opposition parties to their candidacy, had applied the law, when sanctioning a former military officer for illegally wearing military uniforms to campaign, perhaps the electoral result would have been different.

Chávez campaigning in a military uniform.

On Sunday December 8, 1998, 11 million Venezuelans are called to the polls, of which, they vote almost 7 million (63%), which, 4 million, stayed at home, or went to the beach, disregarding the future of the country. Many did not go to vote, since all the polls were Chávez's triumphant. And others, they did not go to vote, since they did not care who won.

The Venezuelan, used to participate in the various electoral processes. For example, in 1988, 81% of the census went to vote. In the 1983 elections, 87% of the population went to vote. Already, in the elections of 1993, low to 60%. The Venezuelan, began to stop believing in politics, and his indifference when voting, in some cases, took it as an indirect message of protest to the rest of society.

The final result of the 1998 elections was that Chávez was elected with 3.7 million votes. That is, he was elected by almost a third of the Venezuelans who were called to vote.

From there, the country, signed his sentence, giving the Presidency, a "crazy", who devoted himself to seek a thousand and one ways to perpetuate himself in power.

THE "COMMANDER" PRESIDENT

Chávez takes office as president in 1999.

On February 2, 1999, Chávez attended the Venezuelan Congress, taking office as the country's president-elect. Yet, 20 years after that fact, in my memory echoes that image of the "commander" when making his oath, with a hand on the constitution of the country, and pronouncing those words, with which he announced to the four winds, that already, his regime, started on the wrong foot. He said that "I swear before God, before the country and before my people, about this moribund Constitution ...", with which, it was already understood, that he would make a new constitution at his personal level. Thus, during all of 1999, the issue in Venezuela was the holding of a popular referendum, which was held on December 15, with the result expected by Chávez.

When I say, expected result, well, according to the "official" figures provided by the government, there was only participated or voted a 44% the population. Of that 44%, 71% said yes. In short, of the 11 million Venezuelans called to vote, they only said yes about 3 million. And with this result, Chávez took out a new constitution, where more than half of the population, as in the 1998 elections, preferred to stay at home. I insist ... only less than a third of the Venezuelan population was the one that helped give strength to the regime.

It draws a lot of attention, that despite the fact that the government itself recognized the low participation, nobody from the political opposition, was concerned about requesting annulment, because the population did not reach a reasonable participation. In many countries, if it is not reached at least 50%, the result is not valid.

One thing that was demonstrated from there, is that Chavismo was interested, in that people did not participate in political life, or in future decision-making. And that, in the long run, what I call the indifference of the Venezuelan, helped to consolidate the regime to some extent.

By the way, Chávez, with the new constitution, introduced a figure never seen in the country: the so-called recall referendum, of which the opposition would try to use it to get Chávez out of power, and in the end, it only served to consolidate "Commander" in the presidential chair. Later, I will tell you the story of the biggest trap created by Chávez, called, a "recall referendum".

Other of the most striking things that brought the new chavista constitution, were the following:

.- The duration of the constitutional periods was changed, which increased from 5 to 6 years, and indefinite re-election was legalized. This created a discussion, since with the previous constitution, a president could not be re-elected, and to be president again, I would have to wait 5 years, in order to be a candidate again. With Chavez, with his idea of perpetuating himself in power, he now had the way open, and could be a candidate, and reelected as many times as he wanted.

.- The name of the Country of the Republic of Venezuela was changed to the Bolivarian Republic of Venezuela. This created some diplomatic incident, since some of the countries in the area, especially Bolivia, felt offended, or threatened.

.- In Venezuela, the V Republic is officially created. From that moment, the regime makes a campaign to discredit everything related to what they call the IV Republic. Unfortunately, that new V Republic, is born with a tragedy, with more than 30 thousand dead.

That December 15, in the morning, occurred in the north of Venezuela, a tragedy. In the central coastal area of Venezuela, during the early morning, heavy rains cause floods and landslides, destroying everything in its path. It was considered the worst natural disaster in the history of the country. According to some calculations, that disaster left some 30,000 dead and more than 100,000 people homeless.

I remember the images of Chávez before the social media that morning. A journalist asks if the rains could influence the voting process of the referendum, to which Chávez responded, citing a famous phrase of the Liberator Simón Bolívar: "If nature opposes, we will fight against it, and make it obey us". That phrase, still echoes in the memory of many Venezuelans, who after the tragic event, still wonder, as a person, before a situation of announced natural disaster, tries to calm the population, citing a phrase of Simón Bolívar.

The reality is that Chavez, whether it was raining, with an earthquake, or a tsunami, he had to win in his constitutional referendum. And nothing, no one, could stop him in his crazy race to perpetuate himself in power.

15-12-1999

Official announcement by Chávez "misinform-
ing" about the tragedy of Vargas.

Many have been the voices that accuse him of having let the tragedy happen, without taking the measures to evacuate, or help the people who lived in the areas affected by the rains. Still, many wonder, where are the weather reports, which could have been avoided, thousands of deaths. Moreover, that same day of the tragedy, at night, Chávez announces in radio and television station, that by that moment, the death toll was 37 people, and that he, had had in his hands , the weather reports, which an-nounced heavy rains. At no time during his chain, wanted to as-sume some responsibility, and only made a triumphant speech about the outcome of the constitutional referendum, stressing that a new V Republic was born. The question is that this new

Fifth Republic would be born marked by a humanitarian tragedy, in which the government, to some extent, had its hands stained with blood.

In the end, the official position of the Chavez government, about the humanitarian tragedy, is that everything was the fault of nature. That is to say, from that moment, it was established bluntly, that the government, is never to blame for anything, and if there is any culprit, that is the political opposition, the wild nature, or the US.

And on the subject of the meteorological reports that Chávez himself had recognized on the radio and television that had been in his hands, well, that was forgotten, and the political opposition, on the other hand, did not take advantage of the situation, to ask for responsibilities to President Chávez himself. If this tragedy happened in another country, surely at least the president would have dismissed him as incompetent, or even worse, he would have been imprisoned for letting 30,000 people die, knowing beforehand what could happen. Imagine there is an announcement of a hurricane for Election Day, and the president, having in his hands the weather reports, decides not to do anything, since for his personal criteria, nothing will happen, and his main concern, is to win at all costs the elections that had already rigged in advance. A, and if something happens, the fault has not been his, if not the wild nature.

THE HIDDEN IDEOLOGY OF CHÁVEZ

I remember some of the "crazy" statements before winning the 1998 elections, where he swore, that he was not a communist, and that he was a deep democrat. So democrat, that he led years before, two military coups, with the result of numerous deaths and woundeds. And I wonder ... maybe people could not see the contradiction of their statements ?.

First encounter Chávez Castro in 1994.

It caught my attention, that he just got out of prison in 1994, one of his first actions, was to make a trip to Cuba in December of that year, where, Fidel Castro, received him with honors of visit from a chief of State. This fact was disseminated by the media, and the people saw it as a curious anecdote. Nobody saw the fact, that Chavez went to bow down to his master. From there, I understood that Cuba would be an undeniable part of the future of Venezuela.

In short, you do not have to be a fortune-teller or an expert in politics to see where the shots went in 1994 and where Venezuela was headed.

I still remember many friends, who voted blindly for Chavez, who told me back then, in 1998, that with Chavez, things were going to get better. Many of them, I answered back then, how is it possible, that among so many candidates with professional training, one third of the country support a person, that their only contribution to society, is to have participated in two military attempts with the result of death and destruction. I told them that if they were choosing a head of a military barracks, I would not even choose Chávez, even though he was a military man.

It was enough for 2 years of "Bolivarian revolution" to pass, so that those fervent friends who admire Chávez would say to me, "Damn Fernando, you were right!"

A DEFINITION OF THE CHAVISTA IDEOLOGY

When Chávez appeared in the world of politics, heading the so-called Bolivarian Movement 200 in 1992, his discourses revealed that his ideology was deeply nationalistic, but with a mixture of left ideals, militarism, and pseudo patriotism. In his first moment, many people saw him with a certain sympathy, since in his speech, he would utter phrases like that he would do justice, and that he would put the corrupt politicians in prison. In those days, he categorically denied that he was a communist or socialist. He defended the free market. Of course, never presented a government plan where he drew what would be their direct lines of action on the economy, or strategic alliances.

All that changed after assuming power in 1999. He began little by little, to take off the mask of a democrat, and to copy the Cuban ideological model, implying that his new project was to develop the blissful "Bolivarian revolution". From the beginning, his goal was always to find ways to reach and remain in power, and to expand his ideology in different countries. Thus, he assumed the role of pseudo dictator, controlling all the powers of the State, and the lives of the people.

One of the first things he did, copying the Cuban model, is to look for a culprit of the evils. And that culprit was anyone who does not think or support the revolution. First they were the so-called "escualidos" (anyone who does not think like him), and from there, began to define very clearly their enemies, or rather, the enemies of the revolution and the country: Media, parties of the opposition, employers, unions, etc. In short, Chávez created two blocks in the country: Those who are with him, and the rest.

The next thing was to set up a super centralized state model, creating types of structures where the new state controls everything, above all, ordinary citizens. To do this, politicized at will the productive apparatus of the country, the judiciary, education, create their own paramilitary organizations, etc.

And so, in 20 years of Bolivarian revolution, we arrived at the "prosperous" Venezuela desired by Chavismo ideologues. Let's see, I'm sure you'll think that how is it possible that the basis of an ideological project is to destroy a people and lead them to total misery. Well, to explain them better, I am going to tell you an anecdote, which could define very clearly the basis of the Chavista ideology:

The Soviet leader Stalin, one day presided over a meeting with his comrades, and one of them, he asked, what was his secret to be a great communist leader. To answer that question, Stalin requested that a hen be brought to him, which he later grabbed hard with one hand, and with the other began to pluck it. The chicken, desperate for pain, tried to escape, but could not. So Stalin managed to remove all the feathers, and told his present comrades: "Now watch what is going to happen." He put the hen on the ground and walked away from her a little, and grabbed a handful of wheat in his hand while his comrades watched in amazement as the hen, scared, sore and bleeding, ran behind Stalin while he was throwing fists wheat and was spinning in the room. The hen was chasing him everywhere. Then, Stalin looks at his comrades, who are totally surprised, and tells them: "That's how easy it is to govern the stupid. They saw how the hen chased me despite the pain I caused him. So are most of the people, persecute their rulers and politicians despite the pain they cause them by the simple fact of receiving a cheap gift or some food for a day or two".

Undoubtedly, Chavez and Maduro have perfectly copied Stalin's idea of how to be a great communist leader in Venezuela: The more hunger and misery people go through, the longer I will be in power. A, and without forgetting another small detail: All the dome of Venezuelan State power (a small group of privileged Chavistas) is rotten thanks to corruption, with more dollars and euros in their bank accounts in Andorra or Switzerland.

Anyway, that's what the so-called populists are like. They ask the rest of society to go hungry and miserable to defend an ideology, and then, those "revolutionary leaders" in their private lives, they spend the money of our taxes at their hands. I still remember what the "commander" Chávez said in full ideological apogee in 2005: "Being rich is bad, it is inhumane. I say this and I condemn the rich. " Such deep ideological thinking has penetrated, that in 2018, the top Chavista leaders (ministers, mayors, advisors, etc.) have more dollars in their pockets, than 5 or 20 years ago. By the way, the family of "Comandante" Chávez, in 2018, is one of the richest in Venezuela, with a diversity of properties and land. It is believed that the "clan" Chávez has a fortune of more than 500 million dollars. Just one detail: one of the daughters of the "comandante", María Gabriela, is one of the five richest women in Latin America. And all thanks to the revolution!

In short, populists (understand: chavistas, podemistas, Sandinistas, communists, socialists and similar), that of being rich, at the cost of killing the people of hunger, for them, that is not very bad. Well, according to its principles, it is only bad, for those who do not think and act like them.

MY FIRST PERSONAL EXPERIENCE
IN CHAVISTA VENEZUELA

At the beginning of July 2000, I went from Madrid to Caracas to visit my family. I found a somewhat different Venezuela, in full electoral campaign, where the Chavistas, announced that if they lost in the next elections, an authentic civil war would occur. In that pre-war environment, I had to walk through the streets of Caracas.

I remember, I found a couple of friends, both linked to a political party, of which some call, from the Fourth Republic. That party is the Movement to Socialism (MAS). One of those friends was Pompeyo Márquez, a veteran political leader, who started out as a communist in his youth, and who, with the passage of time, and disenchanted, understood that this ideology would not work in Venezuela. In the 70s, together with other leaders of the moderate left, they created the MAS. After Chávez's "pardon" in 1994, his party, the MAS, began to consider the idea of giving support in the 1998 presidential elections, with which Pompeyo formed part of an internal front within his party, for stop that support for Chávez. In the end, the Chavista current triumphed within the MAS, and Pompeyo, along with other leaders, such as Teodoro Petkott, in 1998 decided to leave the organization, and from outside the MAS, both decided to confront Chavez and his policies.

Going back to my meeting with Pompey, he greeted me, and asked me what was my life ?. I told him I was studying journalism at a University in Madrid. He answered me, that to go so far, when in the Central University of Venezuela (UCV) I could take the title. I replied that my idea was to obtain a foreign degree, with plans, to dedicate myself as a foreign correspondent. Pompey, he looked at me, and he says: "Boy, congratulations! Very good idea! As things are going in the country, we are going to need many war correspondents!". A short time later, I could see with disbelief, that Venezuelan journalists, went to the demonstrations in the streets,, with bulletproof vests, anti-gas masks, and helmets to play baseball on their heads, as a protection system. By the way, on that trip, I had planned to spend about 30 days in Venezuela, but before the "pre-war" situation that was lived on the eve of an presidential election, on the advice of my family, I decided to leave 15 days earlier than expected.

Pompeyo Márquez, veteran Venezuelan politician.

On July 30, 2000, these new general elections are held in Venezuela. It was done simultaneously with regional, municipal and parliamentary elections. For this reason, these elections were popularly called "mega elections".

Chávez is re-elected for the period from 2001 to 2007. On this occasion, 11 million 700 thousand people were called to vote. Chávez gets 3 million 757 thousand votes. That is, history repeats itself, since one third of Venezuelans vote for him alone. More than 5 million people, did not go to vote.

THE FIRST PROTESTS
AGAINST CHÁVEZ

In that year 2000, the Congress (National Assembly) of Chavista majority, grants special powers to the president. With this, Chávez approves on November 12, 2001, a package of 49 laws, including the controversial land law, which prohibits latifundio.

Many social sectors of the country, hit the cry in the sky before the approval of these laws, for which, the Chavistas in the government, they did not call for consultation to the various sectors of the country at the time of their discussion to reach minimum agreements.

Faced with the eminent abuse of the government, on December 10, 2001, the federation of businessmen Fedecámaras, makes a one-day national strike in protest against the package of laws. Chávez's response to the protest was to call the businessmen "cowardly, immoral," and that he would undertake "tough measures" to stop the protest. He even threatened to take the army to the streets, and decree the state of emergency to silence the demonstrations that day.

It has had to spend barely a year of chavism, for a sector of society to protest the totalitarianism of the government. According to some estimates, the strike reached 90% in the country. For the business sector, the objective of this strike was to "rectify the government, and not destabilize the country." The strike was also joined by the workers' center of Venezuela (CTV) and some opposition parties. All of them agreed, that with the 49 decrees laws of the government, centralism is deepened, It is reinforced expropriations, and faces private property, and increase free enterprise clashes.

On the other hand, already the media of the country, begin to launch their criticism, before the threat of Chavez, to announce, that prepared a law of information content, to impose "ethics" in the media, and deal with to what he considers "an outrage of the truth" by the media. The question is that many of these media, between 1996 and 1998, helped Chávez to become popular by spreading his incendiary speeches. That is, they have had to spend almost three years of Chavez government, so that the owners of these media, they realized, they had committed a fatal error, for having given space and support on the covers of their media, to the glorified image of a dictator in power. I insist ... have had to spend almost three years, for media owners, open their eyes, and began to consider, that Chávez was looking for a long time a "gag law" with his belligerent attitude to the press.

In 2001, several editors and journalists had denounced the government before international press human rights organizations, due to the limitations that existed on freedom of expression and the right to inform. And I wonder ... and why did not they report him in 1994, when he was released, after having planned two militarys coups with the result of destruction and death?

It turns out that between 1994 and 1998, many of these media, businessmen, unions, or individuals, bet on Chávez. Many who bet on that character, knew where he came from, what he did to try to get to power, and what his goals were. It is not necessary to be foolish, to understand, that an active military man, who conspires to give a military coup, his future pretensions, is not precisely, to create a country with a stable democracy. I insist ... the first thing he did after being released in 1994 was going to Cuba to bow to Fidel Castro. And with all this, even someone, three years after coming to power, had doubts about what Chávez wanted for the country ?.

THE FAKE MILITARY COUP OR-GANIZED BY CHÁVEZ

On April 9, 2002, a new general strike was held in the country. On this occasion, businessmen and unions are mobilizing before President Chávez's decision to dismiss a group of non-Chavistas managers of state oil company Petróleos de Venezuela (PDVSA). The commander had announced it in full transmission of radio and telecast, as a threat to anyone who does not go with their ideas..

One of the things that characterized Chávez was his total imposition of going appear on radio and television, to inculcate indirectly, his ideology. He used to appear it was in the prime time (when the soap operas were broadcast), and the usual programming was suspended. Of course, the television stations were not very friendly to give their spaces for free to the government publicity, when it caused them millionaire losses, since at the peak time, and on a radio and television station, advertising could not be broadcast. And this, Chávez knew perfectly well, that with this, he was looking for a way to bend the media. Also, I believe in some sectors of society, some rejection, because many people, at 9 o'clock at night, arrived tired at home, and wished to see a soap opera to relax. But when turning on the TV, they could only see their commander giving his crazy revolutionary speech

The strike begins at 6 in the morning, and the government responds, throughout the day, with the interruptions of radio and television programming on 16 occasions, until 4:00 in the afternoon, make it difficult for private audiovisual media to report on the mobilizations of the opposition, and the evolution of the strike in the country. The government, by imposing such chains, sought to give its monolithic version, that the strike had failed. And on the other hand, by interrupting the programming, it was sought that the media could not report on the strike. For the first time in the country, a government tried to impose its truth, using a method to censor the media.

One thing that impressed me, was how the television stations reacted to be able to inform. The government demanded, that in the case of a chain of radio and television, they had the obligation to transmit that chain live. So, to face the government's strong hand, the private media, then, premieres the modality of dividing the television screens into two windows, to inform about the strike, while still issuing the official version of the television network government. That is, the citizens could see on the screens of their televisions the two Venezuela: the chavista official speech announcing that the strike was a total failure, and on the other hand, see while jointly seeing images of empty companies, and citizen demonstrations in the streets against the government.

In view of the belligerent position of the government, the workers announce to prolong the strike 24 hours more. And Chávez's response was to organize a demonstration in support of his revolution, where he gives a speech of what I call incendiaries, with the slogan that "Venezuela is not stopped by anyone!".

The street protest was held in Caracas in front of one of the headquarters of PDVSA. Chavistas and opponents began to face violent acts. The municipal police are displacing the Chavistas, while the opponents continue in a vigil in front of the PDVSA headquarters with the slogan: "Not a step back. Out! ", And in parallel, there are demonstrations in favor of the government in the center of Caracas, and in some cities of the country, where it predominates the slogan chavista " They will not pass! ".

Before the policy of radio and television networks, by the Executive, private television stations reiterate their decision to divide the screens of televisions, showing in one half, the chavista chain, and in the other what happened in the vicinity of the headquarters of PDVSA in Caracas.

I believe that in no country in the world, where a dictatorship abuses power when trying to manipulate the truth and the media, the media, as is the case of television stations in Venezuela, have faced such dictatorship, risking to report on the truth of what was happening in the country, splitting the television screens in two. When I saw it, the only sound that was issued at the time, was the government chain, announcing that in the country, no one was protesting, and it was enough to see the other image, without the background sound of origin, to understand, that in Venezuela, something happened. At that time, as a Venezuelan, and as a journalist, I felt proud that in the country, a majority sector of society, was moving, and that many people were not willing to be trampled under a dictatorship.

Television screen in two windows, to inform about the strike, while still issuing the official version of the government chain.

The famous April 11, 2002 arrives. On that day, a pacific opposition march, tries to reach the government house in Caracas, and is attacked by gunfire by government supporters. The death of 19 people precipitates the "supposed" military discontent, and a group of generals demands the resignation of Chávez.

I remember with stupor, the images distributed in all the media of the world, as Chavistas shot from the Carmelitas bridge in Caracas. Public opinion abroad was unanimous in condemning the Chavez government. Before this tragic situation of death and destruction, sure, something had to happen in the country.

On April 12, at 3:45 in the morning, in national chain of radio and television station, the military chief General Lucas Rincón Romero, surrounded by all the high military command, and in front of a hundred national and foreign journalists, announces to the country, that in view of the unfortunate events that occurred "the President of the Republic was asked to resign his office" which he accepted ", and whichand that Chávez had voluntarily surrendered and was in custody.

Chavistas shooting at opposition demonstrators
on the Carmelitas bridge in Caracas.

General Lucas Rincon, the day announcing the resignation of Chávez.

Several versions circulated about said resignation request. The first version, is that Chávez himself, made a kind of draft of the resignation, and that later, they made another in typewriter, which, he had also signed. That is, there are two documents announcing his resignation with his signature.

Before the power vacuum, on the 13th, the President of the Federcámaras business group, Pedro Carmona Estanga, is sworn in as interim president, and in a single decree, dissolves the institutions and restores the old official name of Venezuela. That is, overnight, in less than 24 hours, it was intended to eliminate 4 years of Chavistas structures already embedded in the powers of the state, including the army.

The question is that Venezuelans, faced with the supposed fall of Chávez, nobody went out to celebrate. Moreover, those the Chavista followers, they went out to the streets asking that their leader return to power. The issue is that many antichavistas, did not see with good eyes the new substitute of

Chavez, and people, preferred to stay at home to see what could happen.

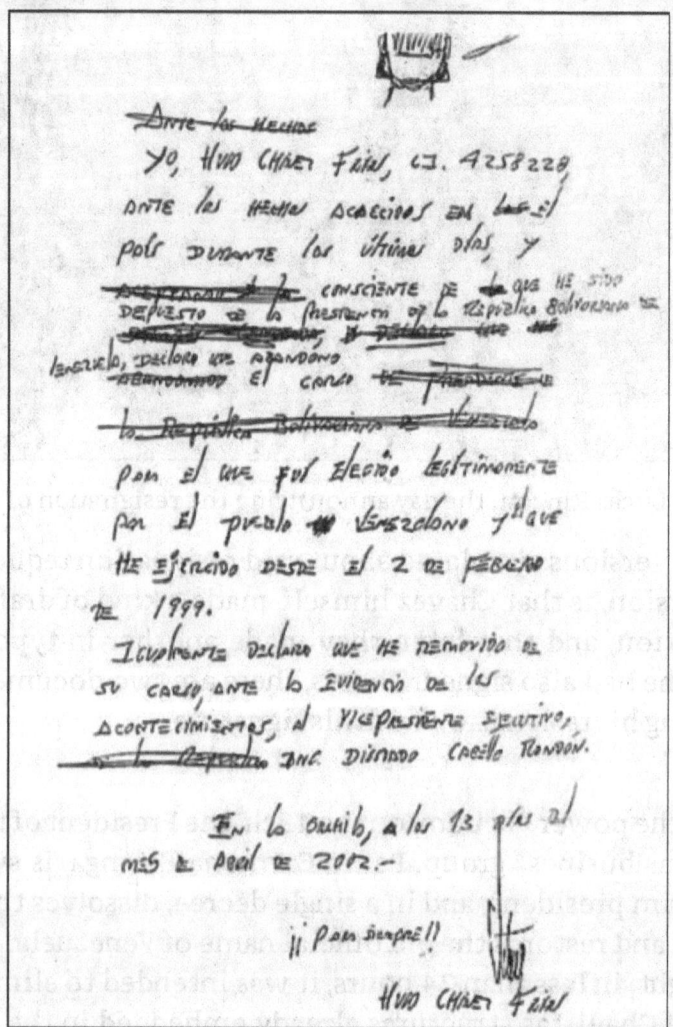

Draft of the famous resignation letter signed by Chávez.

I remember that day, in Madrid, a friend of Spanish origin, congratulated me, and before my curiosity, I asked him the reason for it, and he told me, that I should be happy because Chávez was no longer in power. I answered him, that in reality, I did not feel happy, since Chávez was still alive. The face of my friend was amazed, and he says ... "Fernando! And why do you say that bar-barity! " And I said, "Friend, Chávez alive, he's more dangerous than dead." The next day, my friend told me ... "Fernando, you were right!"

Well, it happens that on the 13th, the Chavista military high command, seeing that Chavez's fall did not come off well, de-cided to stop Carmona for usurpation of functions, and the next day, on the 14th, the same militarys who had announced that Chávez He had resigned from the presidency, they put him back in power.

In short, after a thorough analysis of the facts, there are those who point out that all this was a kind of self-coup mounted by Chavez and the militarys, where the military high com-mand (which Chávez himself chose), was willing to participate in all this show supporting a new supposed government, with the purpose of bringing to light, all those possible antichavist conspirators, both civilians and military, who wanted to form a new anti-Chavez government. And precisely, that's what hap-pened. The question, is that who in the end had the decision power, was that military high command, who knew very well how to act in that situation. That is, after placing Carmona as the presumed president, and seeing who supported him in that "paper government", they proceed to arrest him, and all his al-leged accomplices.

Regarding the issue of the resignation of the "commander", many things have been written. For example, it is said that after his alleged arrest, within the military high command, there was a diversity of criteria regarding the fate of Chávez. One group requested that he be imprisoned and prosecuted for his crimes; and another group wanted to send him into exile in Cuba. On this last option, they say that Chávez had asked for it as one of the conditions to sign the resignation.

Much has also been written about whether Chavez legally resigned. If after his return, that return was legal or not. Whether or not there was a self-coup. The question is that whatever happened in those days, Chávez managed to get out stronger, and what is most unfortunate, is that the murders occurred on the 11th at a peaceful demonstration in Caracas, where 19 people were killed by gunfire of snipers of the government, all this, according to the government, It was a crime, or a plot, organized by the sectors of the opposition.

Months after what happened, I was able to visit the Carmelitas bridge in Caracas, where a group of Chavistas on April 11th fired at the demonstrators of the opposition. In that place, I saw with disbelief, that the Chavistas, had mounted, a kind of altar, to glorify the revolution chavista, guarded, by a group of "revolutionary" followers, with their berets and red shirts.

By the way, General Lucas Rincon, the military who announced the resignation of Chávez on the radio and television, a few months later, was replaced in his post as Minister of Defense and decorated, and later, he was appointed Ambassador in Portugal.

And I still wonder ... how is it possible, that if a group of high military officers, made Chavez resign, and was "supposedly" retained, or imprisoned, and a day later, those same militarys, put him back in the power, and here nothing has happened ?. Well ... I say that nothing has happened to the "alleged" military coup, that with his act, encouraged the "fool" Carmona, to proclaim himself president, with the blessing of those military, and then, in less than 24 hours of his blessing, the military decides to stop him for misappropriation of functions. And in all this story, who was the usurper of functions? Were not the militarys themselves asking for Chávez's resignation and supposedly retaining him illegally?

Anyway ... I insist ... everything points to that it was a montage orchestrated by Chavez himself, and the unfortunate thing is that after what happened, someone still believes that all the fault lies with the "fool" Carmona.

After the "supposed" return of Chávez to power, the instability in the country did not stop. The issue is that under international pressure, Chávez agreed to initiate "allegedly" talks with the various sectors of the opposition, and for this purpose, some so-called "dialogue tables" were established between both parties. Yes, with the mediation of the Organization of American States (OAS). In the end, Chavez himself raised the tables for dialogue, as he affirmed "that one could not negotiate with coup leaders". The result of all this was that weeks later, the opposition protests resumed.

Of all this history of the "autogolpe" of Chávez, there is a curious detail, which I think it is worth commenting. On April 11, on the Carmelite bridge, a group of Chavez supporters fired pistols right and left against the opposition demonstration. One of those Chavistas, his name is Richard Peñalver. This man, was condemned for the facts, and later, in 2007, the Chavez government granted him an amnesty. With his criminal record, Peñalver was a councilor in Caracas for the United Socialist Party of Venezuela (PSUV) in 2011. On April 12, 2015, he was decorated by Aristóbulo Istúriz, then Chavista governor of Anzoátegui state, with the Casa Fuerte Order of first class. And what do you not imagine that has been of this character? Well, the last thing that is known is that in April 2018, he requested political asylum in the offices of the Spanish police on the island of Santa Cruz de Tenerife. That is to say, a killer chavista, asking for political asylum in Spain. And with all this curriculum, at the time of making this note, Peñalver is coordinator of the Barrio Nuevo Mission, Barrio Tricolor, in the Anzoátegui region of Venezuela.

And like Peñalver, there are hundreds of Chavistas leaders who have left Venezuela today, with their suitcases full of money, seeking a better life, at the expense of the suffering of the Venezuelan people.

THE PRONOUNCEMENT OF THE ANTI-CHAVEZ MILITARY IN THE PLAZA ALTAMIRA OF CARACAS

On October 22, 2002, a group of active and retired military men spoke publicly against the government in the Plaza Altamira in Caracas. For some, it was like a kind of unarmed military uprising. Day by day, more soldiers joined the protest to reach about 120 officers. And what did the government do? Let the demonstration of protest continue, to see clearly, how many more disgruntled military could identify, and point to his blacklist. The demonstration was supported by thousands of opponents to the regime, highlighting politicians, and even artistic celebrities, who kept the square full at all hours.

Part of a group of militarys who joined the protest in Plaza Altamira.

In the rest of the country, Chavistas groups, especially those that some define as armed groups, which were dedicated to riding motorcycles, organized themselves, to attend peaceful demonstrations by the opposition, and unleash violence. So practically every day, in the country there were violent street clashes between Chavistas and anti-Chavistas. The government defended its violence, and on the other hand, the opposition parties already directly aimed at the resignation of Chávez, and his government in full.

The Plaza Altamira will be transformed into a symbol of resistance to the government. But on December 6, a tragedy occurs. An armed man arrives there, and without saying a word, pulls out a gun, and starts firing into the crowd. Result: 3 people killed and 29 injured. The police, in that moment of the attack, manages to stop the gunman. After being tried, he was sentenced to 29 years in prison. During the trial, he had alleged that he was not the culprit, and that the real culprit was a television network, for having given coverage to the protesters in the Plaza Altamira. From the story of the character, some things have been written, such as that he was a kind of hit man, formed in Cuba. And what has been the official position of the Chavez government in this matter ?: That the murderer was hired by enemies of the revolution to create a conflict and promote its overthrow.

THE OIL STRIKE

On December 2, 2002, another general strike broke out. On this occasion, it was called "Oil strike", which was promoted by Fedecámaras, the PDVSA board and workers, the opposition parties of the Democratic Coordinating Coalition, the Workers' Confederation of Venezuela (CTV), various organizations such as SUMATE, and the private media.

The strike extended from December 2002 to February 2003, being one of the longest general strikes in history in Venezuela. The chavistas define the strike as "oil sabotage" or "oil strike".

The issue is that Chávez wanted to get his hands on one of the companies, which was at the time, one of the most profitable in the world, and senior officials, and managers, were adamantly opposed to politicizing the company.

Chávez denied that something was happening in PDVSA. But things became too evident, when, on December 5, the crew of the Pilín León tanker declared itself in absentia, and anchored the vessel in the navigation channel of Lake Maracaibo. The ship had just arrived from Cuba, where they had left the first shipments of crude, of what would be the delivery of 100 thousand barrels free to Cuba. The crew of the ship, after verifying the terrible quality of social life, and moral of the communism in the island, decided to support the strike. The captain of the ship, Daniel Alberto Alfaro, had stated that "on the island adolescent girls prostitute themselves for soap or toiletries ... I do not want that kind of life for my daughters". All this before the serious shortage of basic products and food on the island (Venezuela 20 years later). To all this, the controversial statements were added where Chávez affirmed that "we will sail in the same seas of happiness as Cuba ...".

Along with the Pilín León, other vessels that transported oil and its derivatives, from the extraction wells to the refineries, or from these to the distribution points, or to other countries, followed their example.

And what was the response of the government ?: accuse oil employees of committing sabotage against the company PDVSA.

The issue is that from there, the regime realized that it would not be easy to politicize and manage PDVSA at will. One of his controversial decisions by the government was to stop providing maintenance and investment to its facilities, and above all, to make life impossible for those who did not support the Bolivarian revolution within the company.

Consequence of government policies: The performance of PDVSA was severely affected in the following years by decreasing its production, and significantly increasing the number of work-related accidents. They have reached such ridiculous extremes, that the Venezuelan government has even been forced to import gasoline from Brazil, by the bad performance of PDVSA, under their hands.

As an anecdote, I have a cousin who was an official at PDVSA, an engineer who did doctorates abroad, and with unblemished professional training. He told me that they made his life impossible in his work, so that he would resign his position, and with that, lose his benefits by not being able to retire in the company. He told me that every time the government organized a support event for Chavez, they were forced to sign up on a list of attendance at these events. Then, those who did not sign up were part of another black list, which they published on the company's news bulletin boards, so that everyone would know, who was not a Chavista, and with that, the new Chavistas directors, They knew what attitudes to assume in front of those people, with which, I insist, they made their lives impossible. In the end, faced with constant threats, my cousin gave into to such pressure and left the country with his family.

The case of my cousin, is one of the thousands, and thousands of Venezuelan officials, who were persecuted and harassed by the government. The example of PDVSA, was practiced in all the instances and organisms of the State (ministries, state companies, mayorships, governorates, universities, army, etc). As of the year 2000, a wave of Venezuelan professionals begins to leave the country thanks to the ideological persecution. By the way, I still remember a statement made by Chávez about those people who left the country. He even said that these people "were like rats, they leave the ship".

In short, the government created a mechanism to clean up, and expel from the institutions, anyone who did not square, or was a member of Chávez's party. One of its causes of the oil strike of the year 2000, was to denounce the attempts of the government, to put directors and high positions, many of them, without the most minimum experience, or professional formation. I imagine, that now, you will understand, because today PDVSA, is the only oil company in the world, which has lost mony, and have multimillion-dollar debts with Russia and China.

The oil strike ended on February 3, 2003, without further notice from its leaders. A fact that gave the end of the strike, was the occupation of Pilín León, by government forces. Some 30 heavily armed soldiers were responsible for occupying the ship. Of the version of what happened, is that of the captain of the ship Moruy, César Vicente, where he affirmed, that the Pilín León, It was occupied by staff "of Hindu nationality, with suitcases and everything, and also of the National Guard (GN), armed and without the captain's permission." For his part, the defense lawyer of the crew, José Luis Alcalá, who was taken by force from Pilín León, had indicated that, in addition to Hindus, there would also be Arabs and Cubans. "There are more than 50 men who are foreigners, and the president (Chávez) did not get qualified and certified Venezuelan personnel." And so, the example of Pilín León, was applied to the rest of the ships, and the rest of PDVSA.

And what happened to the life of the organizers of the oil strike? Well, a few days after the end of the strike, Carlos Ortega and Carlos Fernández, presidents of the CTV and Fedecamaras respectively, were charged as alleged perpetrators of the crimes of treason against the fatherland and civil rebellion. Faced with this similar accusation, the two fled the country.

MY TRIP TO CARACAS IN 2004

At the end of July 2004, I went to Caracas to visit my family. On this occasion, from my short stay, I took more impressions, than the previous year. For example, one of them has to do with the Caracas metro.

After its inauguration in 1983, I was a constant user for more than 10 years, and for me, as a Caraqueño, as well as for the rest of citizens, it was one of our most emblematic treasures.

I remember that more than one psychologist, did interesting studies on the behavior of the citizens inside the metro. During its first 10 years of history, when a user entered its facilities, the Caracas citizen became a model citizen, who did not throw papers on the floor, gave the seat to the elderly, and respected the basic rules of user, one of the best meters in the world at the time. Nobody stepped on the famous yellow line!

But after the arrival of the "revolution", the metro, it got worse.

During my stay in 2004, I took more than one unthinkable memory of the subway. While I traveling inside one of the wagons, in the middle of the trip, the driver announces by the speakers that they have to stop the train, since there is a "bomb threat" announcement. Yes ... a bomb in the subway !. So I was forced to get off the subway like other travelers, and resign my-self, with all my anger and indignation.

Another thing that impressed me about the subway at that time, was when being inside a subway car traveling to a station, in the middle of the journey, at the Plaza Venezuela station, they enter the subway car asking for alms, three children al-most semi-naked, with hardly each wearing a shorts, shirtless, and barefoot. At that time, I asked a person who was sitting next to me where those children are coming from, and he told me that they are children that are drugged using cans glue, that is, street children, who used the money raised, to buy cans glue to keep drugging.

In short, things such as those experienced in the subway, encounters between Chavez demonstrators or non-Chavistas in the street, and announcements by the government, that if he lost the recall referendum on August 15, in the country, he would to explode an authentic civil war, they forced me, that my planned trip of 30 days to be with my family in Venezuela, was reduced to 15, before the fear, of what could happen. In short, it was the second time, that because of the "revolution", I was forced to leave the country 15 days before the scheduled time.

THE REFERENDUM TO REMOVE
CHÁVEZ FROM POWER

On February 2, 2003, the political opposition held a collection of signatures for a consultative referendum, which was subsequently declared null by the National Electoral Council (NEC) for failing to comply with a series of legal requirements. That night, the opposition celebrated the success of the collection of signatures, signatures that since then were used by the Chavez government to create the first great "political Apartheid" in Venezuela, which consists of not giving employment, state aid, or allowing the entrance to any state or military entity, to the persons that were identified as signatories of the request for an advisory referendum.

The recall referendum was included in the new Chavez constitution, but according to the law, it had to be carried out in mid-2004, and the opposition was not willing to wait that long. In addition, opponents did not accept the conditions of the recall referendum, and requested the referendum of opinion or consultative, which even when it was not binding, required fewer signatures to be convened, and could be done in a much shorter time. The government never accepted the referendum proposed by the opposition, but the one specified in the Constitution. Another difference of criteria in the negotiating table between both sides was the functions of the OAS and the Carter Center. Chavismo spoke of facilitation, while the opposition insisted on the role of mediation.

As I have indicated in a previous occasion, Chávez invented the figure of the recall referendum, with the purpose of consolidating himself more in power.

One of the norms that was indicated for this call, is that the president, had to have fulfilled more than half of the mandate to be convened.

The opposition parties fell into the trap, and they had to swallow, or rather, put up with Chávez, while he outlined that, in order to hold a referendum, the opposition had to present a number of stuffed leaves, with names, number of identity document, signature, and the fingerprints of the signatories. Come on, that just missing, ask for a photo, or video, of the moment of signing.

Collection of signatures to request the recall referendum.

So, all the opposition, mobilized, and the ways of asking for signatures, were very diverse. The places of collection of signatures were placed in public places, such as squares or streets. Volunteers walked house by house in search of signatories. Citizens who wanted to sign, had to do so in books specially designed for that purpose. I remember that in Madrid, and other cities in Europe, the Venezuelan community abroad campaigned to collect the signatures.

In August 2003, approximately 3.2 million signatures were submitted, but these were rejected by the NEC. The excuse is the opposition in a legal technicality: that the signatures had been collected prematurely, specifically, before the middle of the presidential term.

In November 2003, the opposition collected a new set of signatures, obtaining in a maximum period of four days the amount of 3.6 million. In February 2004, Roberto Abdul, one of the directors of SUMATE, the NGO that collected the signatures, declared that according to the calculations of the organization, at least 8% of the signatures (0.288 million) were invalid. However, the NEC rejected the petition for a referendum, arguing that only 1.9 million of the signatures were valid, 1.1 million presented serious doubts, and about 0.5 million were completely invalid (because they belonged to deceased, minors and foreigners). Of the signatures considered doubtful by the NEC (1.1 million), 876 017 had their personal data written in the same handwriting with the exception of the signature itself. The opposition alleged that these signatures, called assisted, were signatures in which the person in charge of the collection center assisted the signers by filling in all the information, and then indicated where to sign. The decision of the NEC, gave rise to violent demonstrations, which resulted in the death of 9 people, 339 arrests and 1200 injuries.

After an appeal to the Electoral Chamber of the Supreme Court of Justice (SCJ) of Venezuela, the court included as valid about 800 thousand signatures, bringing the total number of valid signatures to 2.7 million. This amount constituted 300 thousand signatures more than those necessary to call the referendum. However, a week later, the Constitutional Chamber of the same court rejected the decision of the Electoral Chamber ruling that it had acted outside its jurisdiction.

Eventually, as a compromise to resolve the impasse created, the NEC ruled that it would allow a "repair" process, consisting of allowing for a period of five days in May 2004, those people whose signatures were being questioned, to confirm that if they were in authentic effect. At the end of this period, the number of signatures validated by the NEC reached the figure of 2,436,830. In this way the minimum amount of signatures needed to call the referendum was reached.

In the end, the happy referendum was held on August 15, 2004, and the result was as follows:

Of the 14 million Venezuelans summoned to participate, only 69% vote. Of that 69%, a 59% vote in favor of Chávez, with which, the opposition, was ridiculed. By the way, from there, Chávez declared himself "socialist".

And as for the list of the signatories that supported the referendum, it was published on the internet, and it was known as the "Tascón List" on a personal website of the Chavista deputy of the National Assembly Luis Tascón. Whoever appeared on that list was considered an enemy of the revolution, without rights to anything, and persecuted, not to say, banished from his rights as a Venezuelan.

The president of the CTV, told the Associated Press news agency that they had started to dismiss from government ministries, public bodies, municipal governments, and government companies, those people who had signed the referendum petition. Chavez Minister of Health, Roger Capella, had also declared to the Associated Press, justifying the dismissals, saying that "all those who signed to activate the referendum against President Chávez should be dismissed from the Ministry of Health."

But the persecution against those who appeared on the list went much further. For example, a friend, who had a construction company in Caracas, for years, participated in tenders, to carry out government works. One day, after participating in a process, an official tells him that, unfortunately, he could no longer participate in the projects. My friend, with a worried face, asks the official, which was the reason, and he responded, indicating that his name appears on the Tascón list, and which had been vetoed. So, that thousands of Venezuelans, if at some point in their lives, they needed some procedure, subsidy, help, or whatever, before anything was granted, the government would see if the interested party was on the list.

Fourteen years after these events, the Inter-American Court of Human Rights ruled that the Tascón List was a case of political persecution and violation of human rights. And what has the Chavista government said? Well, that Court, is not competent to interfere in the internal affairs of a deeply democratic country.

THE CREATION OF A NEW ELECTRONIC ELECTORAL FRAUD SYSTEM

Now, one of the innovative things, in the referendum process of 2004, was the application of a voting automation system. That is to say, machines were used, with a computer system, guaranteed, authorized and paid by the same Chavez government. And I wonder ... I being a member of the opposition parties, and after killing myself in collecting millions of signatures, and fighting to recognize those signatures, in the end, I would accept a voting system, which Deduce, what is manipulated by the government?

In short, Chávez set up a whole system, to perpetuate himself in power. He created a way to get free from his enemies, a list of people, which would be persecuted, or lose their rights as citizens. And to top it off, he set up a voting system, where the government itself would be responsible for guaranteeing, and giving its own results.

Moreover, having the Tascon List, with names, surnames, and document numbers, and fingerprint, it is easy that on the day of the elections, with computer programs, the vote of those people could be manipulated. And front that possible reality, and knowing it in advance, the opposition openly accepted, that this voting system will be implemented.

The NCE, or rather, the Chavez government, hired the services of the Smartmatic company, which was run by two Venezuelans in the US.

For the day of the referendum, and subsequent future elections, they use in all the voting tables, "modern machines", which are rented to a Spanish company. These machines have a reader, where the person, who wishes to vote, has to put his finger, and the machine is connected to a telephone line, which connects with the headquarters of the NCE, and electronically validates the voter. Subsequently, the person can cast their vote, through the option of pressing on a touch screen, the desired option (Yes or No), and then, the machine, printed a piece of paper, with the indicated option, and then, the tiket with the printed result, was entered into a voting box.

Models of voting machines used in Venezuela.

He drew a lot of attention, that within the scheduled operation of the voting process, although there were ballot boxes, where the alleged votes were introduced, in polling stations, after closing the tables, those boxes with the votes were never opened, , and if they coincided completely, with the result of the lists with the total results, which were printed. Their results, were based only on what the computer program totalized.

In principle, with the idea of avoiding a possible fraud, or mistakes of the voting process, it was established that, at random, after the closing of the polling stations, and inside the voting center, some ballot boxes would be opened, to verify that the information of the result of the minutes coincided with the votes of the polls. But, this, never came to fruition. That is to say, before this fact, the opposition, could have requested the annulment of the process. In fact, they filed some kind of complaint, but in the end, Chávez, got away with it.

What did NCE do in the face of this alleged irregularity in the audit of the votes on the day of the vote? Three days after the vote, I insist, three days later, at the headquarters of the NCE, an audit was carried out with some ballot boxes, of which, there was no guarantee, that they came from any of the 8,141 voting centers. That is, the same chavista NCE, was, who set up, audited, judged, and sentenced, that everything was correct. The origin of the voting boxes used in said audit was never certified.

From the Smartmatic company, hand hired by the Chavez government for the voting processes, many things have been said. For example, that of its first three contracts with the Venezuelan government, it took out about 120 million dollars. Or that seven months before the referendum of 2004 was organized, he secured from the Venezuelan government a loan of 200 thousand dollars, guaranteed with 28% of the shares of a company linked to Smartmatic.

According to Smartmatic, they offer services of biometric systems for registration and authentication of voters, electoral identifications, software and electoral services, computing and transmission of results, administration of electoral days, and online voting.

But everything has not been perfect for them. Several of the elections in which he has participated, such as the Philippine presidential elections of 2010 and 2016, have been marked by criticism of the security of Smartmatic's systems, and even by accusations of fraud.

In his years working in Venezuela, Smartmatic says that he has deployed more than half a million electronic voting machines and trained more than 380,000 operators. The company ensures that its system is designed so that, in case of manipulation, its detection is immediate and very easy to identify thanks to the installed audit mechanisms.

But everything changed in 2017, when the company decided to denounce that the elections to the National Constituent Assembly on July 30 of that year, with which Nicolás Maduro, intended to draft a new Constitution to suit, and abolish the opposition Parliament, allegedly said Elections had been manipulated. If ... for the first time, after participating in numerous voting processes in Venezuela, using practically the same electronic voting system, with the same machines, now, Smartmatic, affirms, that the Venezuelan government had made a fraud, since there was "Manipulation of participation data".

According to the managers of the company "the difference between the amount (of votes) announced and the one thrown by the system is at least one million voters".

Smartmatic, according to them, "between 2004 and 2015, organized 14 elections (...) and processed more than 377 million votes in Venezuela", in addition to the controversial election of the Constituent in 2017.

And after 15 elections, now they come with that story ?. It is curious that in 2005, they did not say anything about how the NCE inflated the number of participation in parliamentary elections.

Those parliamentary elections were held on December 4, 2005, where 167 deputies to the National Assembly were elected, 12 deputies to Parlatino, and 5 deputies to the Andean Parliament.

On that occasion, and with the background of the previous elections, the opposition parties refused to participate, in what they called, another "electoral fraud" with the machines. According to the same government, there was a census of more than 14 million voters, and they only went to vote 3 million 604 thousand. That is, the same government, indicates that only 25% of the people went to vote. That is, according to the same government, 75% of voters stayed at home.

Thus, on that occasion, the Chavista theory was perfectly fulfilled, that if people lose interest in participating in the electoral processes, this is very good for the revolution. In fact, I think that in spite of everything, the NCE manipulated and inflated the number of participation, since the same opposition, denounced that in the voting centers, the participation, was very inferior to 25%. But anyway ... if it was 5 or 25%, that not matters. With only the participation of Chavez parties in the electoral process, it was possible for the Chavistas to obtain an absolute majority in Parliament.

And what should the opposition have done before a fraudulent electoral process? Very simple: Order your followers to deposit null votes on the day of the elections. You imagine an election, where the null vote been the absolute majority ?. Well ... only that could happen in Venezuela. So, for the next, gentlemen of the opposition, take note of the idea.

A, also the lords of the opposition, could take the example of a region of Brazil, where in 1958, they chose a certain Cacareco, as governor. And do you know who Cacareco is? Well, it was a hippopotamus zoo in Rio de Janeiro. Unfortunately, the poor man did not take office for which he had been elected, since his 100 thousand votes were canceled.

THE GAG LAW

In November 2004, the National Assembly of Venezuela, with a Chavistas majority, approved the Law on Social Responsibility in Radio and Television, known as the " Gag Law ". The owners of the media, and the opposition, considered it a "gag" that "restricts freedom of expression" in the country.

Despite international criticism and condemnation, Chavismo was clear that, by controlling what the media published, they could spread their version of the truth of what was happening in the country. Later, in 2005, this law came into force, with the approval of new regulations imposed on the media, which stipulated heavy fines, and even jail in case of defamation of public figures (Chavistas).

With the rise of Facebook, and other platforms in the network of networks, Venezuelans ventured into the Internet, to find out what was happening in the country. But this did not last long, since in December 2010, the Chavistas approved a new "gag law" for the control of the Internet and social networks. Thus Venezuela becomes part of the exclusive club of countries that like China, Iran and Cuba, control cyberspace.

THE BIG BUSINESS WITH RUS-
SIA AND CHINA

In July 2006, after the announced US arms embargo In 2005, Chávez signed an arms deal with Russia for three billion dollars, including an agreement for the acquisition of Sukhoi fighter jets, and helicopters, in what it meant, a move away from the supplies of US weapons. In addition, it also acquired about 100 thousand Kalashnikov assault rifles. The question is that there are some details of the "big business", which even today, present serious doubts.

After the fall of the Soviet Union, Russia, it was found that in its stores, they had a large amount of weapons, and equipment, obsolete, that were literally rotting. So, one day, Mr. Vladimir Putin, he learned that there was a country full of oil, with a "revolutionary" political leader and a great enemy of the US. And Mr. Putin said ... that's my client ! So the diplomatic mechanism was launched with the aim of reaching trade agreements, and as a result, Russia committed to deliver about 24 combat aircraft, and some other things. And everything in exchange for ... millions of barrels of Venezuelan oil. Let's see if I explain: At the time of signing, Venezuela offered 3 billion dollars, money that Venezuela does not have physically. Thus, Chávez mortgages part of the oil reserves to the Russians, as a guarantee of payment. And from there, future business with Russia and China, are made with the payment of oil not yet exploited or extracted from its underground deposits.

To get an idea of good business, in 2017, Venezuela signed a debt restructuring agreement with Russia, where Venezuela would pay Russia a total of 3.15 billion dollars over a period of 10 years.

Chávez and Putin.

According to the Institute of International Finance, in 2017 Venezuela had an external public debt of about 150 billion dollars, including 45 billion dollars in government liabilities, and another 45 billion dollars in PDVSA debt.

As for China, for about 10 years, Venezuela signed several agreements, executing more than 780 projects with an investment of more than 50 billion dollars. China has granted credits to Venezuela worth 62 billion dollars in those 10 years. Of that money, Caracas, en 2017, must still return some 20 billion with oil supplies. Another detail is that since Venezuela has not been able to pay the debt with that country in the last three years, China agreed to only charge interest. Part of those interests were collected in 2017 with 700 thousand barrels of oil per day. I insist ... that 700 thousand barrels a day for a year, is only the payment of interest on the debt with China.

And meanwhile, despite the billions of dollars lent to the country, the population goes hungry, there are no supplies in hospitals, there are no medicines, the electrical infrastructure is rotten with thousands of blackouts ... Let's see if anyone Do you understand ... And all that money, where has it gone?

And to top it off, in 2018, Maduro dedicated himself to continue doing business with the Russians and Chinese to borrow more money. The problem is that even though Venezuela has the largest oil reserves in the world, the Russians and the Chinese have begun to doubt that the business is profitable, and more, when there is a risk, that Maduro will one day fall, and instead, a successor arrives who does not recognize the debts with those countries.

Maduro during his visit to Beijing, with the president of the National Petroleum Corporation of China, Wang Yilin.

In mid-September 2018, Maduro went to Beijing to ask for more money. If ... a president who in his government has spent and wasted thousands of millions of dollars, went on a business trip to find a new loan of 5 billion dollars. Maduro, with the same speech as always, reiterates that Venezuela has enough oil to pay the new debt.

Various sources claim that the Venezuelan government has offered its untapped reserves of natural gas, and gold, as an additional guarantee. That is to say, at the rate that Maduro is going, in five years from now, China and Russia will own all the oil, gas and gold reserves of the country, while hunger has killed more than half of the country.

Several NGOs have denounced for years, how the Venezuelan jungle is being deforested, thanks to the invasion of gold prospectors, who pollute the rivers with mercury. That is, today, there is a gigantic lack of control over mining, and to top it all off, Maduro thinks to say on his trip to China that "there are financing commitments for the growth of oil production, the growth of production of gold and investment in more than 500 development projects within Venezuela. " Gold production ?. If friends and ... we already have the Chinese miners looking for gold in the jungle of the Amazon, and everything they get, they will take it to China, as part of the payment of interest on the debt created by the Bolivarian revolution. Yes ... the interests of the debt! We must not forget that the mining infrastructure in Venezuela is in worse condition than the oil industry. In short, what the country will have is a greater growth of uncontrolled deforestation in its Amazon rainforest, with greater contamination of mercury and other toxic substances in the earth, air and rivers, and everything in return, that Maduro, got thousands more millions of dollars, to be squandered on scams, such as the purchase of millions of tons of food expired abroad.

As a curiosity, I am going to tell you one of the many businesses that were made between Venezuela and China. At the end of 2015, Maduro inaugurated with solemnity in Venezuela, a Chinese plant to produce buses. The idea was to produce about 3600 buses every year, with an investment of 275 million dollars, which have come from a loan to China. According to sectors of the opposition, the real price of that project was more than 900 million dollars. And in the end that has been of that factory? In 2016, of that large number of 3600 buses planned, according to figures from the same government, only 600 were produced. And in 2018, how much was the production figure? ... To the incredible number of 0. To this, adds another small detail. From the arrival of Chavismo to power, Venezuela until the year 2017, bought about 7 thousand new buses manufactured in China. For this, it spent about 1200 million dollars. According to sectors of the opposition, the real price of each bus is about 80 thousand dollars, while the government had paid 179 thousand dollars for each, with which there is an over cost of almost 100 thousand dollars per bus. And where did that money end up? ... More than the doubt of where the money went, the question is to know what happened to those 7 thousand buses. According to several mayors where these buses had been destined, the vast majority, rest in abandoned junk bus cemeteries, since the government, as a good negotiator, had acquired a type of transport not suitable for Venezuelan roads, full of holes, with which, those buses broke down easily, and when there were no spare parts, they went straight to the cemetery of damaged vehicles.

By the way, since the beginning of 2018, in Caracas, as there is no public transport, because the fleet has been deteriorating like Chinese buses thanks to the lack of spare parts, a new type of transport has emerged, which they popularly call "kennels". Yes ... literally, they are cages with 4 wheels, where people travel standing up, enclosed like animals huddled together by others. They are large vehicles like trucks, to which they have placed bars as cages. Thus, today Venezuelans travel: In cages with 4 wheels. There are those who compare that situation of public transport with Cuba. The issue is that at least, in Cuba, today they use second-hand buses sent as scrap from Spain, where in that country they do not circulate according to safety regulations. That is to say, in Cuba they use vehicles that have been withdrawn from circulation in Spain because they are obsolete, with which some businessman he makes his big business, and takes them to the island.

Part of a cemetery of Chinese buses in Venezuela.

One of the popular "kennels" circulating in Caracas in 2018.

I leave the Chinese business a little, and I'm going to tell you something about Russian business.

In relation to the purchase of the first Russian fighters, there is the anecdote, that the Venezuelan pilots, experts all their lives, in piloting American F16 fighter aircraft, took their hands to their heads when they received the news that they were going to pilot Russian planes. In fact, those pilots were sent to Russia to receive training, and after their return to Venezuela, we would say, they had not outgrown the training. But the doubts about the formation of these pilots, was in the air, when on September 17, 2015, one of these Russian planes fell to the ground, dying its two occupants. The official official version of the government of the cause of the accident was the weather. Although, later, there was some high government official, who had come to affirm, that the plane was attacked and shot down.

In mid-2018, the Venezuelan NGO, Citizen Control for National Security and Defense, presented a report on the air accidents that occurred in the Bolivarian National Armed Forces during the 18 years of Chavismo. Despite the opacity of the Venezuelan State, which has been dedicated to hide, or manipulate the catastrophes to not justify the victims, the NGO revealed that since the year 2000, there were 72 air accidents, with more than 160 people dead.

In the report, 24 incidents are reported, with the balance of 89 deaths. These statistics correspond mostly to helicopters of Russian manufacture Mi-17V-5, belonging to the Army component. The second place is occupied by transport aircraft with 23 accidents, combat aircraft with 15, and finally, training aircraft, with 10 accidents.

The NGO explained in its report that catastrophes "are the product of lack of maintenance, damage, failures in the doctrine of training by some components, and even flight indiscipline."

On the other hand, the NGO highlighted that accidents had decreased, since the government had not been concerned, for giving adequate maintenance to its military equipment, with which, a direct consequence was the decrease in the number of missions, and On the other hand, faced with the imminent danger, the pilots looked for some kind of excuse not to fly, for example, a medical leave. That is, if today, a pilot forced him to get on a plane, or helicopter, the safest thing is that he would refuse to do so, on the understanding that it would put his life at risk, and that of many more.

The Venezuelan military pilots, know very well some cases, such as the one occurred on May 3, 2009, when a Russian helicopter model MI-17 falls in the Venezuelan region of Táchira, and leaves a balance of 18 soldiers and a civilian dead. Or the case of another MI-17V-5, which rushed to the ground on May 18, 2012 in the Army Airfield Colonel José Joaquín Veroes, with the tragic balance of 4 deaths and one injured.

But as the NGO says, there are possibly many more cases, which have been covered by the government, or their consequences have been minimized.

Russian helicopter crashed in Venezuela on February 5, 2019 with the balance of 5 injured.

In July 2010, a K-8W crashed in northern Venezuela.

The issue is that within the opposition, there are those who affirm that the weapons acquired from both Russia and China are scrap, or material, that does not exceed quality controls.

China has also sold "junk" to the Venezuelan army. To give an example, between the years 2010 and 2013, three "new" K-8W Chinese-made aircraft, acquired in 2010, have crashed in the country. In this case of the three Chinese aircraft, the pilots were able to escape unharmed, self ejected.

PRESIDENTIAL ELECTIONS OF 2006 AND THE NI-NIS

For December of 2006, other presidential elections are organized. One thing that caught my attention, was the figure presented on the level and participation, which according to the government, was 74%. That fact made me doubt a lot, since the tendency was that participation was on the downside. A year before, in the elections to the Parliament, 75% of the registered population, did not go to vote, because in its immense majority, it did not believe in a clean elections were given. But in the case of 2006, this increase in participation can only be explained, as there was certainly some kind of manipulation to "touch up" the figures. I insist ... from one year to the next, the population can not change their opinion about an electoral system that, as time went by, was getting worse.

On the other hand, the opposition, which had always criticized, and denounced frauds, on this occasion, decided to participate in the Chavista "circus". An example of this circus is that 22 presidential candidates were presented, a number of candidates that had never been seen in the country.

Of all of them, Chávez's main rival was the Governor of Zulia state, Manuel Rosales, who temporarily left his position to participate in the electoral process. It had the backing of a coalition of 43 types of political organizations, highlighting the main opposition parties, compared to the 24 organizations that supported Chávez.

Another thing that caught my attention in this process was the appearance of the so-called "ni-nis". That is, people who did not support the two candidates. In fact, a third candidate had emerged, who had the sympathies of the so-called ni-nis, but one month before the elections, he had to resign as a candidate, due to health problems.

In the end, Chávez achieved his victory with 62% of the votes, while Rosales only achieved 36%.

THE PERSECUTION TO FOREIGN COMPANIES AND THE CONSOLIDATION OF 21ST CENTURY SOCIALISM

On January 10, 2007, Chávez is sworn in as president, and announces that the main energy and communications companies would be nationalized. That is, he announced his intentions to nationalize the electricity companies of Caracas and the Compañía Anónima Nacional Teléfonos de Venezuela (Cantv), as well as the passage to the State of the control of oil refining in the Orinoco Oil Belt, and that the Central Bank of Venezuela (CBV) would cease to be autonomous.

He had also announced that he would ask the National Assembly to grant him special legislative powers with the enactment of an Enabling Law that would allow him to take "revolutionary" measures to advance, what he had called, "the socialism of the 21st century".

In June 2007, two US oil companies, Exxon Mobil and Conoco Phillips, refuse to give most of their control of their operations in the Orinoco Oil Belt, and the government proceeds to expropriate them. The contradictory of all this history, is that shortly after, the Russians and Chinese, would take control of many of the oil facilities of the country. That is, with the excuse of nationalization, the Chavistas protected in the supposed spirit of revolutionary Bolivarian struggle, confiscate companies some, then sell, or do business with the confiscated, with others (Russians and Chinese), with the idea of take out billions of dollars from their "new owners", and then steal all the money.

The Orinoco Oil Belt is a territory with an extensive area rich in heavy and extra-heavy oil, with a total area of 55,314 km² and an exploitation area of 11,593 km². This territory is considered the largest accumulation of heavy and extra-heavy oil in the world. The original oil reserves on the Faja site, according to PDVSA, amount to about 1.36 trillion barrels. That is why both Chinese and Russians want to control this area.

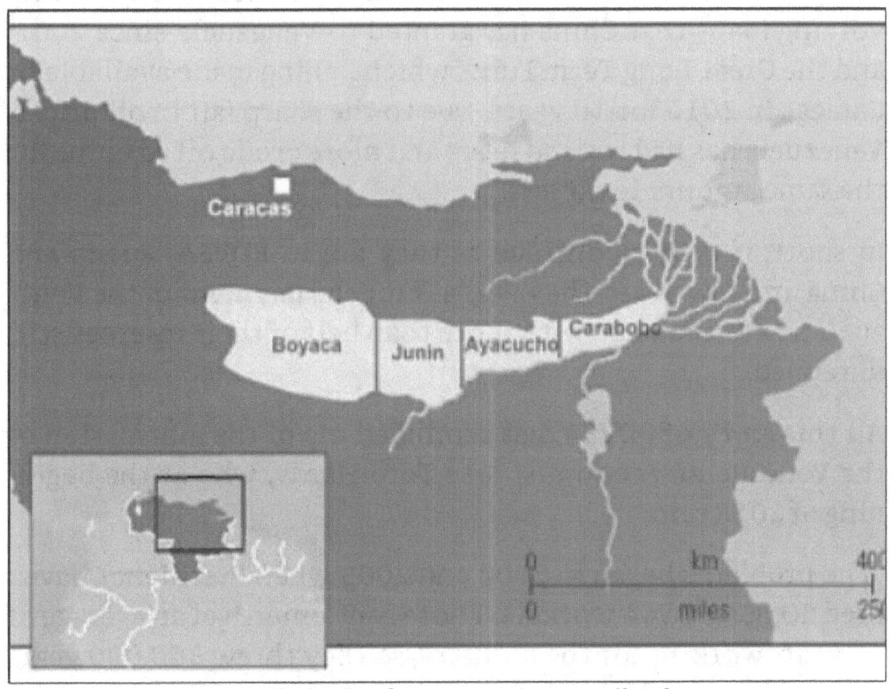

In yellow, the famous Orinoco Oil Belt.

Already in 2018, and after one of those many agreements, where the Russian company Rosneft, was going to manage the Amuay refinery with a capacity of 650,000 barrels per day; and Petro-china, which would manage the Cardón refinery, whose capacity is 310,000 barrels per day, at the end, both companies decided to take a step back, upon discovering that Maduro wanted to deceive them, by offering them a Venezuelan oil industry with abandoned infrastructure and practically destroyed, and that to raise it, it would be necessary to assume multi million dollar investments.

On the other hand, in mid-2018, Russia and China receive 70%

of profits from associations in the Orinoco belt. Both countries charge with oil the debt that the Chavez government contracted with them to finance fiscal spending, which reduces Venezuela's income from oil exports.

The crude oil sent to China is mainly destined to pay the revolving loans that China has granted to Venezuela since 2007, and the Great Long Term Fund, which Beijing made available to Caracas in 2010 for 10 years. Due to the sharp fall in oil prices, Venezuela has had to send more and more crude oil to China for the same amount in dollars.

In short, if things continue as they are in PDVSA, Russia and China, in a few years, they will ask for the payment of the Venezuelan external debt with more than half of their reserves still untapped.

All this story of PDVSA, has reminded me of the affirmation of the Venezuelan economist José Toro Hardy, who at the beginning of 2018 said:

"The problems began in 2002 and 2003 when President Chávez fired 20,000 PDVSA workers. Those gentlemen had an average of 15 years working for the industry, so they threw 300,000 years of experience and knowledge into the garbage basket. "

And those people who were fired, engineers with doctorates, master's degrees, specializations made in various universities and prestigious academic institutes all over the world, in the end, were replaced, by Hindus, Russians and Chinese, who did not have the slightest idea of how it works a refinery

Therefore, it is understood that the Venezuelan oil company, went from being the second or third largest oil company in the world, to become the largest "administrative disaster" in the world.

As an anecdote, everyone knows the agreement of Cuba, where Venezuela changes about 80 thousand barrels of oil per day by Cuban doctors service in Venezuela. Well, in September of 2017, the government of India signed an agreement with Venezuela to change medicines for oil. As far as I know, more than a year has passed since that agreement, and nobody has seen in Venezuela, any medicine "made in India". In fact, for years, there are no medicines of any kind in Venezuela. People who have chronic diseases are having a very bad time, and thanks to the solidarity of some NGOs, some medicines arrive from the outside, but they are very few. By the way, nobody knows the barter conditions of Indian medicines. It is possible, that in about 10, or 20 years, we find out, that Venezuela has exchanged 50 thousand barrels of oil, for 50 boxes of aspirin.

THE RCTV CASE AND THE PER-SECUTION TO THE PRESS

In May 2007, the Chavez government refused to renew the broadcasting license of the RCTV television channel (Radio Caracas Televisión), because it was critical of President Chávez. The closure of the channel announced by the government, generated protests in the streets and against the closure of the television plant, and a strong international condemnation. Already on December 28, 2006, the "commander" had announced the closure of RCTV. And of course, not to renew the concession, was an excuse, and a warning, for the other media.

On the other hand, in the case of RCTV, some Venezuelans media, such as the Globovisión television station, came out in their defense of RCTV, alleging, among other things, that the RCTV concession he expires in the year 2021. But who can question the word of " commander"?. If he says that it is February 30, 2018, and that in that year the month of February has 28 days, then, the calendar in Venezuela is changed, and ready!.

The hypothetical story of changing the calendar is not a story. Already the "commander", in 2007, changed the time use of Venezuela, to be the only country in the world, which instead of having an hour of difference as do the rest of the countries of the world, was passed to 30 minutes. A total royo, and everything to come out in the international press. In the end, at the beginning of May 2016, Maduro, decided to return to the old schedule, with the excuse, to save electricity. The truth is that long before 2016, Venezuela is experiencing constant electric blackouts, thanks to the terrible state of the electrical installations.

Returning to the RCTV case, on Sunday May 27, 2007, at 11:59 pm, he stopped broadcasting. Immediately after the signal of the channel was extinguished, the Chavista government seized the broadcasting equipment of the station to transmit, minutes later, the signal of a new state "public service" channel called Tves. And I wonder ... Tves, would have gone on the air, without the need to seize the RCTV transmission equipment? Well, surely not. Chavez already had in mind long before December 2006, the idea of looking for a way to set up a new television channel, confiscating technical equipment from a television channel contrary to their political interests. So it occurred to him, not to renew a concession of a television channel, using as an excuse, that the conclusion that ended in 2021, ended in 2007.

Undoubtedly, the RCTV case, at the time, was one of the battle horses of the opposition to Chávez. Since the intention to close the channel was announced, thousands and thousands of Venezuelans demonstrated in the streets, in defense of freedom of expression. But the mobilization of citizens, both on the street, meetings with international organizations, condemnations on the part of the international community, or heads of other governments, did not help.

Eight years later, on September 7, 2015, the Inter-American Court of Human Rights (IACHR) condemned the Venezuelan State, and ordered it to re-establish the frequency to RCTV, alleging that "In the present case an indirect restriction to the exercise of the right was established to the freedom of expression produced by the use of means designed to impede the communication and circulation of ideas and opinions ". And to all this, what has the Chávez government done before said condemnation? ... Well, disregard all the condemnations and criticisms.

After RCTV, his next victim, would be Globovisión. That if, instead of confiscating the transmission equipment, the government did something more bizarre. In May 2013, a "business group" made up of militarys, linked to Chavismo, bought that television station, with which its previous anti-Chávez editorial line went down in history. The new president of the company, Juan Domingo Cordero, from the first day he took office, devoted himself to an ideological cleanup, dismissing all that journalist not friend of the regime.

For many Venezuelans, Globovisón was the only window left to a democratic society. His position against denouncing the irregularities of the government earned him the nickname "Plomovisión". The work of the journalists of the chain, when it came to covering some type of news related to the government, was of real value, including, risking their own lives. On more than one occasion, reporters were assaulted by Chavista groups, or their equipment had been destroyed, or stolen. They lived day to day, watching their backs, as they were constantly threatened, with phone calls to their homes. Undoubtedly, for me, they are true fighters to get the truth, and to defend freedoms.

Finally, in dictatorial regimes, one of its main goals is to end freedom of expression, either confiscating transmission equipment with the excuse of not renewing a concession, or creating dubious "business groups" to buy means at prices Far below the market, thanks to blackmail or threats. In fact, in the case of Globovisión, who fixed the price was the government, but yes, warning the previous owner, that they were not going to give him the licenses for digital television, with which, if he did not sell, he would be the only one channel in analog signal in Venezuela. And of course, of that it is worth having an analog channel, in a digital world. Moreover, if they had followed an analog signal, sooner than later, the government would look for some other way, to buy the channel at a lower price.

But the case of the television, is not a separate case in relation to other media.

In the case of the printed press, well, at the beginning of

Chávez's arrival, he sought a very subtle way of controlling the written press. Newspapers, in order to get their product out on the street, need to buy paper, ink, and other types of supplies, abroad. Being products from abroad, you have to obtain import permits, and most importantly, process the purchase of the dollars before the same government, since unlike in other countries, there is total exchange control of foreign exchange in Venezuela. That is, the government is the one who says and decides, who has the right to get dollars.

Many media, such as the newspaper El Nacional, or the newspaper Tal Cual, have been assuming the role of RCTV, or Globovisión, to be the paladins to denounce the irregularities of the government.

On the other hand, many print media, live on the advertising of various advertisers, and in Venezuela, one of those advertisers, is the government, which conditions such means, in the sense that the less you speak ill of the government, the government will reward you with more advertising space.

But since the arrival of the Bolivarian revolution, dozens of print media have been forced to close and fire people. If the government does not give paper import permits, or the dollars to buy that paper, it is impossible for them to get ahead.

There are some, such as the case of Tal Cual, an openly anti-Chavez newspaper, which in spite of the persecution to its owners and workers, succumbed to the fact that they could continue making the printed version, and they have had to keep working leaving in web page format. But despite changing the format, the persecution persists. I know the case of a journalist from that media, who at the end of 2016, one day they called his house at night, and they threatened him, that if he did not leave the country in 24 hours, they would arrest him and his family. So, as he could, he grabbed his family, and practically, with what he had on top, he left home, and left the country, with fear in his body. Like him, many other journalists have had to leave the country, before the constant threats of the followers of the "revolution".

The newspaper with the highest national circulation in Venezuela, the Últimas Noticias, had the same end as Globovisión. This newspaper, was part of the Cadena Capriles (today Grupo Ultimas Noticias), where other print media were edited, such as the newspaper El Mundo. That is to say, after numerous pressures from the Chavistas, the Capriles chain was sold at the beginning of June 2013 (a few days after Globovisión), to a mysterious business group. That mysterious business group had named the deputy chavista David De Lima, as president editor, and in turn, president of what would be the new business group, and with it, he was the one who decided that, or not, could be published. From then on, the covers "Maduro says", "Maduro promises", "Maduro will put a hard hand", became daily bread. So the Last News, which was known as "the newspaper of the people", would become an official propaganda organ of the Presidency of the Republic.

As for who owns the group, the official version is that it was acquired by the British investment bank Hanson Asset Management. The question is that according to Decree 2095, dated February 13, 1992, in article 26 of the chapter on the sectors of the economy reserved for national companies, it is established that:

"The following sectors of economic activity are reserved for national companies:

a) Television and radio broadcasting; newspapers in Spanish. "
Thus, according to Venezuelan legislation, the sale of Cadena Capriles, to a British company, is illegal.

To this, we must add article 9 of the Venezuelan telecommunications law, which prohibits foreigners from acquiring media.

In short ... if someone Chavista high circles, wanted to mount a story to justify under the rope, the purchase of Cadena Capriles, by a group of foreigners, and that additionally, appoint a Chavista political leader, Deputy David From Lima, as the high position of the group, well, let me tell you, that all this, I create many doubts.

What I believe, is the following:

Days before, with what happened with Globovisión, where it had been announced that those who bought the television station were Chavistas, this had created an authentic wave of protests at national and international level against the government. So, if in less than a month, people learn that the government has bought the chain with the largest newspaper in the country, insurance, that the protests would multiply. So, they set up a whole plot, to say, it was a British group, to ward off suspicion. But when the Chavista David De Lima is appointed as the highest authority, already Globovisión was old news, and what happened with the Cadena Capriles, well, was something that was in the background, unimportant.

In the case of the Cadena Capriles, the Chavistas, who had violated two Venezuelan laws, which forbade the sale of media to foreign companies, were so ill-prepared.

A, another detail of the story: Those non-Chavistas journalists, who worked at the Cadena Capriles, as well as Globovisión, and some radio stations that "bought" or "confiscated" the Chavez government, were persecuted and pressured in their Job positions. That is to say, they wanted to impose the new official editorial line, and many communicators, faced with their professional ethics, resigned from their jobs, and those who tried to put up with their in jobs, in the end, were dismissed.

By the way, regarding the future of Globovisión, there is still nothing written. In 2012, the news channel had to pay a fine of

2 million one hundred thousand dollars to prevent their transmission technological equipment was confiscated by the government.. The media regulator imposed a fine on the channel for the coverage of riots by prisoners in Venezuelan prisons. Well, it must be emphasized that the government had approved an information content law, which established, for example, that television channels could not transmit violent content during their broadcasts. This was done by the government on purpose, to apply a mechanism of prior censorship of information content, since for example, if in any city of the country there was any demonstration against the government, and this was violently repressed by the security forces, that information, by law, could not be transmitted on television, since according to the government, this type of information contains violence. In the case of the prison riots, the government applied its law, on the understanding that Globovisión broadcast content with violence.

NEW CONSTITUTIONAL RE-FORM IN 2007

In November 2007, a campaign was launched for a Project to reform the Constitution, promoted by Chávez, with the purpose of modifying 69 articles of the 1999 Constitution, among it is established that Venezuela is a Socialist State. Another proposal was to increase the presidential term from six to seven years, and also allow for continued reelection. In addition, it gave him control of foreign currency reserves, the central bank, the territorial organization of the country and greater powers to expropriate property, or censoring media in emergency situations.

On December 3 elections are held to approve or reject the constitutional reform, with a result that some would call a heart attack. The No, win with 52% against the Si, with 48%.

After recognizing his first electoral defeat, Chávez called the opposition victory a "shitty victory" because of the narrow margin of two percentage points between both options. Of course, he left a clear message announcing that it had been a defeat "for now", and that he would not rest in his attempt to re-present said reform, to which the opposition went in block, reminding him that the Venezuelan Constitution itself Chavista prohibits that a proposed reform that has been rejected, will be presented again in the same constitutional period.

Thus, in spite of everything, in 2009, without having finished the constitutional period, Chávez would try again, that is, violating the same constitution that he created in 1999, to create another one that would give him more powers.

NEW WAYS OF CHAVISM TO ELIM-INATE THE OPPONENT

In November 2008, regional elections were scheduled. But before the date came, Chávez had to find a way to nullify those opposition candidates who had a clear chance of winning.

At the end of February 2008, the Comptroller General of the Republic informed the NCE of a list of disabled persons who can not claim any responsibility for regional elections, based on article 105 of the Organic Law of the Office of the Comptroller General of the Republic and the National Fiscal Control System. Among the disqualified were the candidate for Caracas Metropolitan Leopoldo López, and the pre-candidates for the Anzoátegui, Miranda and Táchira government Antonio Barreto Sira, Enrique Mendoza and William Méndez respectively, as well as other mayoral candidates, including Oscar Pérez .

In short, the Venezuelan opposition considered the list as a political reprisal against that sector.

But all this did not remain there. At the beginning of November, another list of opposition candidates who were disqualified by the Electoral Chamber of the TSJ was released. On this occasion, it was the turn of the former governor and opposition candidate for the governorship of Yaracuy, Eduardo Lapi. And in that environment, the Chavistas announced that the next to fall would be the candidacies for governor of Henrique Capriles Radonski in the Miranda region, and Henrique Salas Feo in Carabobo, as well as that of the mayoral candidate of Maracaibo Manuel Rosales.

The campaign took place in a climate, one might say, pre-war. Every time Chávez opened his mouth to give a speech, he announced that if the opposition won in the most important regions of the country, a civil war would take place.

In these elections, the government created around the parties that supported Chávez, a coalition called "patriotic alliance", where as a result, the agreed candidates, interestingly, were directly supported by Chávez. The Chavistas wanted to give wanted to give an image of democracy when an electoral process was called to choose those candidates among the political organizations that made up this coalition. But in reality, who made the final decision, of who was the candidate for a governorship, or mayor, was Chavez himself.

For its part, the opposition, on January 23, to mark the 50th anniversary of the fall of the Perez Jimenez dictatorship, created the coalition of National Unity, made up of various political parties, with the commitment to present joint candidates in all the states and municipalities of the country. Thus, like the parties that supported Chávez, the opposition organized an electoral process to choose its candidates.

For these regional elections, some 16 million people were called to the polls, of which about 11 million voted, with which participation was around 65%. What does not fit in the results of the accounts, is that Chavez obtained a 52% of votes, which, he had gotten 17 Governorates and 272 mayoralties. While the opposition, obtained 41% of the votes, and only got 5 governors, and 54 mayorships. So, I do not understand, how the opposition gets a result somewhat similar to the government, the Chavistas get 3 times more governorships, and 5 times more mayorships, than the opposition.

After this result was analyzed by the opposition, many have reached the conclusion that on the part of the government, there was manipulation, or electoral fraud. We just have to remember that whoever set up the electronic voting system in Venezuela with machines was the Chavismo.

REFERENDUM OF 2009

On February 15, 2009, another referendum takes place in Venezuela, with the name of the Approving Referendum of the Constitutional Amendment. On this occasion, its end, was to get Chávez's approval of the "Amendment No. 1" to the Constitution to abolish the limits to the terms in office for president, state governors, mayors and deputies to the National Assembly.

A year earlier, Chávez had lost a referendum, where one of the issues was the extension of the presidential term. In fact, the same day he was defeated, the "commander" said that he would try again, which the opposition in a block, he told him, could not do, since the constitution clearly establishes that during In the same legislative period, two referendums about the durability of the presidential period can not be made.

Although there was that clear vice of unconstitutionality, in the end, the opposition decided to participate in the Chavez game.

Once again, the electoral mechanism of the electronic machines powered by the arrival of Chavez was put into effect, and the results were more than controversial:

The Yes reached 6,319,636 votes (54.86%) and the No 5,198,006 votes (45.13%), and an abstention of 30%.

With the "approval" of this new constitutional reform, the Chavism got a way to impose their regime more firmly.

THE CHAOS OF THE ELEC-
TRICAL SYSTEM

In 2010, Venezuela starts the year succumbing to what some define as "electric chaos". That is to say, the blackouts or power cuts in the country begin to be common. And the cause of it ?. Well, very simple. From the arrival of Chavez to power, his main goal was to nationalize the electricity industry. Consequence ... that during more than 10 years of "Bolivarian revolution", the government devoted itself to waste money in helping countries friends and allies of the revolution, and on the other hand, stopped investing in maintenance and modernization of facilities and electrical infrastructures. When the problem was more than obvious, the government, which is never to blame for the bad things that happen in the country, it occurred to him to find a culprit. And that guilty iiiiis ... the weather phenomenon known as the child. Yes gentlemen, the fault is of the nature, and not the bad management in the electrical sector.

Venezuela has one of the largest hydroelectric power plants in the world, the Guri, which generated more than half of the country's energy.

But one of the things that the government does not count on is that Guri has 20 giant turbines to generate electricity, and that in 2010, of those 20 turbines, 7 do not work, since they had serious maintenance problems. In fact, they were turned off, faced with the possibility, that if they let them work, a great tragedy could happen with an explosion.

But Guri, is not the only gloomy thing about this history of blackouts. In that same year 2010, an explosion or fire occurred on October 20 at the Plant Center, a thermo-plant located near Puerto Cabello (Valencia), totally destroyed one of the five generation units. Inspectors of the Directorate of Intelligence and Prevention Services (Disip) were sent by the Ministry of the Interior and Justice, to determine if the explosion and the fire were caused by saboteurs, but the managers and union leaders in Planta Centro said that the explosion with fire, was the result of ten years of almost zero maintenance. But the official version of the government is that it had been sabotage. Well, I think the correct term would be self-sabotage caused by the government itself.

So before the obvious problem of the blackouts, the "commander" decided to declare a state of emergency, with the taking of some measures, something curious.

At the beginning of that year 2010, it was established that during a period of 150 days and until the rainy season returns, the Public Administration would work continuously from 08:00 AM to 01:00 PM. As an anecdote, a few days before this measure, unsuccessfully tried to cut the light for four hours (from 9 to 11 in the morning and from 9 to 11 at night), but the effects of the first day of application plunged into Caracas in the chaos. Schools, medical centers, public lighting and traffic lights were without electricity. Chávez himself ordered his annulment, and dismissed the Minister of Electric Energy, Ángel Rodríguez, who had only been in office for two months.

In short, since 2010, the blackouts have been growing from bad to worse. When it does not rain, they say that is the Meteorological phenomenon "the child". And when it rains a lot, they point out that the fault lies with saboteurs who make attacks on electrical installations. Of all this story, there is one thing very clear: the fault is never the government.

By the way, in 2018, "the child" has not touched Venezuela, and the blackouts, in relation to 2010, had tripled, or quadrupled. So, we deduce, that for the government, the saboteurs, have tripled.

THE FRAUD OF THE PARLIAMEN-
TARY ELECTIONS OF 2010

In September 2010, new parliamentary elections are held. Of more than 17 million people called to vote, only 66% participated, which, in relation to previous parliamentary elections, where the opposition did not participate, due to fraud complaints, in the latter there was an increase in participation of 40 % (This according to the figures offered by the government).

What I do not understand, is like the opposition, knowing perfectly well, that the electoral machinery is managed at will by the government, they let themselves be cajoled, and they participate in the game of fraud.

At an international level, there were countries that considered that these elections were another show organized by Chávez. For example, on July 13, the Chilean National Congress had agreed that a group of senators would be sent "to verify that there is no fraud in that election." And Chávez who said about it ... well, those people were not going to set foot in Venezuela.

Of this electoral process, it draws attention to the following:

The Chavista coalition obtained an absolute majority, 98 of the 165 seats, although it loses the qualified majority of 2/3, which it maintained since 2005. For its part, the opposition, grouped under the coalition Mesa de la Unidad Democratica (MUD), it obtained 33 deputies less than Chavez, although the difference in votes between the two forces was less than 1%. That is, have they had almost the same number of votes, but the Chavistas get 33 more deputies? And how is that ... very simple. Before the elections were called, Chavez promoted a reform of the electoral law, which established rules for proportional vote calculation, where, curiously, in the regions where the opposition is predominantly strong, in those areas, to achieve a Deputy, they had to get more votes than expected, and in other areas, where Chavez is strong, there, conditions were easier to get more deputies. Thus, it is explained, how the government, and with the help of the "machines" on the day of the elections, they mounted their "show".

And meanwhile, the opposition gentlemen, knowing all this, participated in the trap set by the government.

The new electoral law had an important effect on proportional representation. Based on the population data applicable in the parliamentary elections of 2005, the proportion deputy list / nominal was 68/32 at the national level, having regions with a proportion 77/23 (Lara and Aragua) and regions with a 50/50 ratio (Cojedes , Vargas, Nueva Esparta).

With the previous Electoral Statute of the Electoral Power, in its article 15, it indicated that for each state 40% of the deputies will be elected per list and 60% of the deputies in nominal districts.

In the new Chávez electoral law, it does not include the discount between the nominal votes and lists, allowing a political formula that has obtained 31% of the votes, being the largest minority, to obtain 85% of the seats in the Assembly, for a hypothetical example

With the new Law, the NCE has the discretion to form the circuits with combinations of Municipalities, Parishes, Communes or Communal Councils. Although it defines a population index for the nominal circuits, it does not establish that it is mandatory for the NCE, nor with how much time should the districts be anticipated, nor does it indicate the margin of error for these circuits with respect to the index of population. The above opens the door to the NCE to create circuits for political chavista convenience.

This explained, as the Chavistas, presenting a result of votes similar to that of the opposition, with less than 1% difference, get 33 more deputies.

Before the announcement of the results, on September 25, the Venezuelan NGO Súmate, presented an informative preview, in which it concluded, that during the elections there was a "design and control of the electoral system tailored to the interests of the national executive", "Intimidation of actors and voters" and advantage, also pointing out that "from the NCE itself, it is sought for these parliamentary elections that the electoral results favor the government, so that it manages to maintain the majority of the seats in the National Assembly".

A, another important detail in the history of electoral processes in Venezuela: The Chavez government is the one who finances its own electoral campaigns, with economic resources, which are never justified. And not only money, but also infrastructures, media, etc. A clear example of this advantage, are the radio and television channels, or the "Aló Presidente" program, where Chávez has dedicated them to campaigning and insulting the opposition. In short, Venezuela is one of the few countries in the world, together with Cuba, or North Korea, where the government uses all the resources of the state to campaign on its behalf, and to discredit the adversary.

THE DETERIORATION OF THE HEALTH OF THE VENEZUELAN

As the country falls apart, the health of Venezuelans is getting worse. Epidemics, or diseases that had already been eradicated, began to appear, and others, such as tuberculosis, dengue, zika, or chingunguya, would spread.

Gloomy image of a courtyard of El Rodeo prison, full of garbage.

In April 2011, inmates of El Rodeo II Judicial Confinement Center, kidnapped a group of employees of the Ministry of Interior and Justice, including the prison director, to demand attention from the government. The fact was motivated thanks to an outbreak of tuberculosis inside the jail that had not been attended to. After various negotiations, the hostages are released. But on June 12, that is, in less than a month, in El Rodeo I, a brawl broke out, with 26 dead prisoners. The days go by, and the situation becomes untenable. On June 21, a national newspaper published an information, which states that the mutineers in El Rodeo I and II, have Browning M2 machine guns, Beretta 92 pistols, AR-15 and AK-47 rifles, among other weapons Subsequently, on July 5, the government reported that the search continues in El Rodeo I, finding a shipment of weapons buried in a wall of the enclosure. On July 9, the inmates of El Rodeo I deliver 29 inmates of the prison in exchange for food.

In the end, on July 13, more than a thousand prisoners entrenched in the prison of El Rodeo I and II, have surrendered to the security forces.

Of all this tragic history of the prison of El Rodeo, where it is unknown the number of people killed within their facilities, or people who died from tuberculosis, or other diseases, there is no impartial official report that speaks of it. But there is something in which everyone, including the government itself, agree: all Venezuelan prisons, go through a situation of authentic horror story.

On the other hand, in all the hospitals of the country ... yes ... in all the hospitals of the country, there are not the most elementary supplies to attend the citizen. For years, the government has refused to continue providing official statistics on deaths due to diseases, since this would imply, indirectly, recognizing that the country's health system does not work.

Another detail is that for years there are no vaccines, which, the new generations of Venezuelans, have grown totally defenseless against possible outbreaks of measles or diphtheria. If we add to all this the growing malnutrition, and the contamination of rivers and air, well, it is not surprising that there are cases of tuberculosis, or epidemics of measles. Only in the Bolívar state, in the south of the country, in the year 2017, more than 400 thousand cases of malaria were registered, when in 1961, Venezuela had joined the World Health Organization (WHO) as a malaria-free territory. In short, today Venezuela is known as the country where malaria, diphtheria, tuberculosis, measles, HIV and scabies have resurfaced. According to the WHO, by the 2018, malaria is expected to affect more than 900 thousand Venezuelans. And before all this what the government says ?. Well, in Venezuela there is no humanitarian crisis.

And then, if there is no humanitarian crisis, why have Cuban doctors been in the country for 20 years? And in September 2018, officially, Chinese doctors began to arrive. Yes ... Chinese doctors.! On September 22, 2018, the Chinese hospital ship He Ping Fang Zhou (Ark of Peace) arrived in the country to provide medical assistance. The government, through the Minister of Defense, General Vladimir Padrino, gave the news as something extraordinary. Let's go ... of course it's extraordinary, that the government has denied all kinds of international humanitarian aid for years, and now, with the Chinese vessel, well, it turns out that that's something else. By the way, what the minister has not said, is how many millions of dollars it cost to bring that ship, which has only been in Venezuela for a week.

With the "business" of the Chinese hospital ship, the government wanted to imply that they had already solved the country's health crisis. According to the Venezuelan Medical Federation and the Venezuelan Health Observatory, by that time (September 2018) in the country there was a shortage of 85% of medicines and 80% of medical-surgical material. And with a week of stopping a Chinese vessel in a port, the government has solved the problem.

THE USE OF VIOLENCE BY THE REGIME AS AN ELECTORAL WEAPON

On October 7, 2012, presidential elections are held to designate the President of Venezuela for the 2013-2019 term. Chávez wins the elections with 55% of the votes, against 44% of Henrique Capriles, thus achieving the "commander", his fourth consecutive term.

During the campaign for these elections, Chávez encouraged in his speeches to his followers, qualifying Capriles with terms like "Bourgeois", "apatrida", as well as with pejoratives like "majunche" (little thing), "jalabola" (flatterer). For his part, the leader of the opposition, responded to insults, with calls for dialogue and responsibility.

But before the elections, several violent incidents occurred, in which the opponents were attacked, resulting in deaths and injuries. An example of this was what happened on September 2, when four people from the opposition were shot near a voting center where an electoral drill was held, south of Lake Maracaibo. Another violent fact was what happened on September 12, where fourteen people were injured, when Chavismo supporters blocked a highway for which the candidate Capriles planned to reach the city of Puerto Cabello. The worst of the events occurred on September 29, when two opposition leaders were shot dead in the town of Barinitas by Chavistas officials.

In its strategy for fear of losing power, the government gives the green light to the creation of the Immediate Mobilization Networks, a supposed paramilitary organization, presumably created by Chávez, to continue controlling the country should it be defeated in the presidential election. Among its objectives were aborting opposition rallies before they could be prepared, the detection of opposition leaders, the organization of street and resistance demonstrations, and territorial control. Of its approximately 3,800 members, not all would have had military objectives. Some of them were limited to observation tasks. Other functions foreseen for these groups, composed of small teams of between five and seven people, was to encourage violent actions. Sources of the Venezuelan Army had assured that in June of that year 2012, they began distributing some 8,000 AK-103 rifles to this organization.

A large part of the Chavez militias is made up of very old people to which the government gives them armaments, putting their lives at risk.

By the way, already in 2007, Chávez, had already officially created the so-called "Bolivarian militias", which, "are trained to defend the (Bolivarian) revolution of their internal and external enemies."

In short, Chávez throughout the years, a more perfect system was set up than the Cuban one, to consolidate a single idea: to perpetuate himself in power.

AND WHERE DID NICOLÁS MADURO COME FROM?

Well, the official Chavista version indicates that Nicolás Maduro Moros was supposedly born in Caracas on November 23, 1962. I say, supposedly, since after assuming the presidency in 2013, the rumor came to light that Maduro was born In colombia. In a chapter later, I will tell you the story of this "rumour".

As a child, Maduro received classes at the Liceo José Ávalos, in the popular parish of El Valle de Caracas. It is said that his first contact with the policy occurred when he became a member of a student association of his institute. Others say that his father, Nicolás Maduro García, was a trade unionist and active activist of the political party Movimiento Electoral del Pueblo (MEP), and that as a child, he went accompanied by his father to several events of the party, where the Maduro boy never showed interest, since I did not see the MEP as an extreme party, or ultra left.

Maduro with the Sai Baba in New Delhi.

Maduro was raised as a Catholic, although I think he never stepped on a Catholic church of his own free will. In 2012, it was learned that Maduro was a follower of the Indian guru Sathya Sai Baba. However, he declares himself to be a Christian.

Nicolás Maduro's biographer, Roger Santodomingo, said in a report in 2013 that Maduro and his wife, Cilia Flores, "were faithful followers of the guru," and that in his office, it was full of amulets, and that some "came from of Sai Baba ", a person "who only accepted blind faith ".

At age 12, Maduro was already active in a radical leftist organization called Ruptura. Among his ranks was also the historical Venezuelan guerrilla, Douglas Ignacio Bravo Mora, who had participated in the coups military of February 4 and November 27. of 1992. The activity of the group Ruptura, concentrated in numerous actions of shock, such as painted on the street and violent protests.

According to some sources, when Maduro was 15 years old, he was expelled from the high school for putting together a large mobilization. Shortly after, he managed to graduate from high school at the José Ávalos high school, in Caracas, although after finishing high school he did not enter university, and then, he started working on his own.

It is said that in 1983, Maduro worked as a bodyguard for José Vicente Rangel, a left-wing Venezuelan political leader, who at the time was a presidential candidate, and who, years later, in 2002, was vice president of the Republic with Hugo Chávez.

Maduro, already 25 years old, during the years 1986 and 1987, he studied at the Cuban school of formation of left political cadres "Ñico López" in the city of Havana. And all thanks to a scholarship that got him La Liga Socialista, ultra left organization, which was very linked in his time as a student at the lyceum.

They say that during his stay in Cuba, he was very loyal to the ideology of the Cuban revolution, and that some of his teachers saw in him a brilliant future as a disciple of the regime. In any case, since 1986, the Cuban regime had already signed Maduro into its ranks, and the Castro, to a large extent, bet on its future.

Maduro, accompanied by a group of "comrades" during his stay in Cuba in 1986.

The writer Carlos Alberto Montaner, in his article "The Man of Havana", reveals that Maduro began to organize contacts between Chavez and the Castro brothers when he studied at that Cuban school of formation of leftist political cadres. According to the writer, "Nicolás Maduro is much more than a sympathizer of the Cuban revolution or a radical Marxist outcast, platonically in love with communism: he is an old collaborator of Castro's intelligence. That is why Raúl Castro convinced Hugo Chávez that this was his natural heir. Maduro was part of the group. He was one of them", says Montaner.

On the other hand, it is also said that during this stage of ideological formation, Maduro meets Bolivian coca grower Evo Morales, who received political courses in Havana, and who is now president of Bolivia. So, at least, we have two presidents who have left Marxist-Leninist ideological training courses in Cuba.

Back in Caracas, Maduro stands out as a student leader of Maoist groups (ultra left) at the Central University of Venezuela, and although there are no records of his enrollment in that university, some sources claim that he studied for two years in the School of Administration. It is noteworthy, that it was very common, that groups of militants from the ultra left, posed as students within the universities, to organize vandalism, and to look for supporters. In fact, in the years 60, it was a habitual practice of the radical movements of the left, to create chaos within the universities. In any case, Maduro, has never spoken of his supposed stage as a university student.

Maduro, during his time as a bus driver.

On June 9, 1988, in Caracas, he married Adriana Guerra Angulo, and in 1990, his only son, Nicolás Maduro Guerra, was born. The marriage lasted until 1994.

In 1990 he began working as an area inspector in the Metro de Caracas. Later, he found employment as a bus driver in 1991, a position he held for 7 years. During his work as a driver, he began his political career by becoming an unofficial trade unionist representing bus drivers of the Caracas Metro. It is said that he was the driver with more fines for the bad exercise of his profession.

Press conference of MBR-200 members in 1997. Chávez in the center, and Maduro is on the far left.

It is also reported (rumors) that he participated in several attempts prior to the military coup d'état of November 27, 1992 against the government of then-Venezuelan President Carlos Andrés Pérez.

On December 16, 1993, together with a group of workers sympathetic to the Revolutionary Bolivarian Movement 200 (MRB-200), Maduro paid a visit to Chavez, who was being held in the Yare Prison due to his failed military coup attempt.. On one of those visits, he met who would be his second wife, Cecilia Flores. Maduro, since then, became an ultra activist for the liberation of Chávez. After the pardon granted by President Caldera to Chávez in 1994, Maduro, Cecilia Flores and another group of supporters helped Chávez organize his political movement, which culminated in the creation on October 21, 1997 of a new party called Movimiento Fifth Republic (MVR), replacing the MBR-200.

Maduro, as a deputy in 1999.

In 1998, while Chávez was consecrated as a presidential candidate by the MVR, Maduro becomes a candidate for deputy of the old Congress of the Republic with the support of that party for Caracas (Federal District), being elected in the November 8 elections. 1998. In that same year, Chávez achieved his electoral triumph. Maduro took office as deputy on January 23, 1999, and became the Head of the Parliamentary Fraction of the MVR in the Chamber of Deputies, as well as the Permanent Commission for Social Affairs, the Permanent Commission of Social Communication Media, of the Commission Permanent of Youth, Recreation and Sports and of the Permanent Commission of Citizen Participation.

In 1999, he was elected deputy for Caracas in the Constituent Assembly that drafted a new Constitution that same year. In the constituent Maduro presided over the Commission of Citizen Participation, of said parliament, and later was elected deputy to the National Assembly of Venezuela (NAV) in the elections of July 30, 2000 by the MVR. In the NAV he chaired the Permanent Commission for Integral Social Development from August 14, 2000 until January 5, 2005. On January 5, 2005, he was elected to preside over the NAV.

Maduro in his time as president of parliament in 2006.

Maduro was re-elected in the legislative elections of 2005, being appointed as president of the parliament, and in August

2006, he leaves the NAV to later occupy the position of Minister of Popular Power for Foreign Affairs. Curiously, and I say curiously, after leaving the parliamentary activity, his wife, Cecilia Flores, was in charge of replacing him in his previous high parliamentary position.

AND THE ELECTORAL SCAM FOLLOWS

On Sunday, December 16, 2012, regional elections were held. The Chavistas get 20 of the 23 governorates, and parliamentary majority in 22 of 23 state legislative councils. If we add up the total number of votes at national level, we find that the Chavistas, with 56%, take almost 100% of the governorships and of the state legislative councils (regional parliaments). I insist ... with a little more than half of the votes, they have taken more than 95% of the elected positions, without forgetting that from that famous 56% general they got, has been the result of fraud, because without the famous electoral system with the machines, surely they would not have reached 20%.

After knowing the results, some candidates of the opposition, like Andrés Velazquez, in the Bolívar state, raised their protest voice, since the NCE, before counting all the minutes, gave as a winner, the candidate of the chavismo in that region. Velazquez, insisted, that there were about 126 Voting records to totalize, and that if those records were taken into account, he would win by a narrow margin. For 10 days there are peaceful protests in the Bolívar region, and in the end, the Chavismo imposed his candidate.

MADURO: FROM CHANCEL-
LOR TO PRESIDENT

In June 2011, a new political scenario began to be lived in Venezuela, thanks to the diagnosis of the carcinogenic disease that
was detected in the "commander" Chávez, and which required
urgent treatment in Cuba. Maduro, from Havana, was in charge
of announcing, on June 10, the "corrective surgical procedure"
to which the head of state had been subjected several hours ago
following the detection of a "pelvic abscess" that, as it was recognized days later, it turned out to be a malignant tumor. For
Chávez, it was the beginning of a calvary of surgical operations
and aggressive treatments of chemo and radiotherapy that, despite the successive optimistic parts of Chancellor Maduro, and
of the patient himself, did not manage to stop the metastasis
and eradicate the cancer.

The unavailability of Chavez in these months of disturbing
come and go between Caracas and Havana, resulted in a media
coverage of Maduro as chancellor, who replaced the president
in events such as the XXI Ibero-American Summit and the V
Summit of UNASUR, both in Assumption in October 2011, the
VI Summit of the Americas, in Cartagena de Indias in April
2012, and the XLIII Mercosur Summit, in Mendoza in June. This
last appointment had great significance for Venezuela because
it supposed, the approval of the entry of Paraguay, as the fifth
member state.

In July 2012, Chávez, after three surgeries, four sessions of
chemotherapy and six rounds of radiotherapy, said he was
"totally free" of cancer, and confirmed his new reelectionist
candidacy, for the 2013-2019 term, in the voting. presidential
elections of October 7, which ended up winning. During the
electoral campaign, Maduro could be seen driving the truck

from which Chávez greeted militancy a couple of times.

The electoral triumph of Chávez did not dissolve the restlessness that had taken hold of his followers. Despite the official versions that everything was going well, and that the life of the "commander" was no longer in danger, few believed him capable of completing his second term of six years.

Strategically, Chávez activated the succession scenario on October 10, 2012, three days after winning the presidential re-election. On that day, after receiving from the president of the National Electoral Council (NEC), Tibisay Lucena, the credential that proclaimed him president for the period 2013-2019, the president announced the appointment of Maduro as executive vice president of the Bolivarian Republic of Venezuela. As an informal presentation of his eighth vice president since 2000, Chávez stressed that Maduro had been "a great public servant on different battle fronts", and with laudatory irony, said of him: "Look where is Nicolás, the autobusero. Nicolás was a bus driver in the subway, and how they have made fun of him, the bourgeoisie mocks. "

On November 23, 2013, Maduro turned 50 in the midst of a new wave of rumors about Chávez's state of health, which had not appeared in public for several days. The vice president skipped the XXII Ibero-American Summit, held in Cádiz on the 16th and 17th (on behalf of Venezuela was the vice chancellor for Europe, Temir Porras Ponceleón), but did not miss the VI Summit of UNASUR, in Lima on the last day of the month. In between, on November 28, Chavez returned to Cuba to begin a "special treatment" consisting of "several sessions of hyperbaric oxygenation and physiotherapy."

At dawn on December 7, Chavez, with a healthy and cheerful appearance, was back in Caracas. After him, on the runway of the Simon Bolivar International Airport in Maiquetia in Caracas, immediately after the commander's daughters, he appeared descending the steps of the Nicolás Maduro plane with a smiling face. On the following day, from his office in Miraflores, with a more serious tone, flanked by Maduro on his left and by Dios- dado Cabello Rondón, the president of the National Assembly, on his right, Chávez transmitted a momentous message to the nation. First, he revealed that he had been found new malignant cells in the exhaustive review carried out in Cuba, and that the recurrence of the cancer, required his return to Havana in the next hours to be intervened without delay, in what would be his fourth surgical operation since 2011, for which, he requested the Assembly authorization to be absent again.

Given this situation, President Chavez, for the first time, evoked the scenario of an irreversible disability, and pointed to his vice president to supply it: "If, as the Constitution says, some circumstance arose that would disqualify me from continuing in front of the Presidency of the Bolivarian Republic of Vene- zuela, either to end the few remaining days (of the 2007-2013 mandate), and, above all, to assume the new period for which I was elected, if something should happen, I repeat, that disquali- fied me in some way, Nicolás Maduro not only in that situation must conclude as the Constitution mandates the period, but my opinion firm, full, irrevocable, absolute, total, is that in this scenario, which would force to convene presidential elections, you choose Nicolás Maduro as president of the Bolivarian Re- public of Venezuela, I ask you from my heart. "

According to Chávez, Maduro's election was justified, since: "He is a full-fledged revolutionary, a man of great experience des- pite his youth (...), a great capacity for work, for conducting groups, to handle the most difficult situations "(...) He is one of the young leaders with the greatest capacity to continue, if I could not, with his firm hand, with his gaze, with his heart of a man of the people, with his gift of people, with their in- telligence, with the international recognition that they have earned, with their leadership, in front of the Presidency of the

Republic, leading together with the people and subordinating to the interests of the people the destinies of this country. "

Moment when Chávez announces his successor, Nicolás Maduro, who is sitting next to him.

With these solemn words, Chavez designated Maduro, who listened to the words of his superior with a serious gesture. Maduro It was designated as will be the responsible person in charge of exercising the Presidency in case of Chávez do not assume as president before or after January 10, 2013, the day that would begin the six-year mandate granted by the October elections.

Additionally, Maduro would be the candidate to succeed him if presidential elections were to be held within 30 days. It was his reading of article 233 of the Constitution, which established the mechanism of succession of the president Chávez in cases of death, resignation, abandonment of office, dismissal by sentence of the Supreme Court of Justice (TSJ), popular revocation of the mandate or physical or permanent disability mental.

However, the same article, in its second paragraph, stated that in case of absolute lack of the president as an elected or re-elected, before taking office, the functions of the head of the State fell temporarily to the President of the National Assembly, Diosdado Cabello. The legal framework generated ambiguity and Chavismo opted to support the first interpretation of the law, , clearly to save Maduro. It is important to highlight, that the provision contained in article 229, prohibit an executive vice president in exercise (Nicolás Maduro) to run for president of the Republic.

On January 10, 2013, Chávez had to be in Caracas, swearing in his position as re-elected president. The issue is that he could not attend, since he was being held in Cuba undergoing another medical treatment to face the cancer he suffered. On the 10th, the followers of Chávez took to the streets to "defend the Constitution", and that from that day on, the government was still in office with Vice President Nicolás Maduro at the head, on the principle of "administrative continuity".

For their part, the opposition parties insisted that in the absence of Chavez, there is a temporary absence from office, and that this should be assumed by Diosdado Cabello.

On March 8, 2013, Maduro swears in the position.
He is accompanied by Diosdado Cabello.

The problem is that it was the desire of the supreme "commander". And so it rains, thunder, or flashes, Maduro is the substitute, sworn in, or not, legal or not, and point!

But there is not all the history left. When Chavez died on March 5, Maduro took office three days later as head of state and government as "president in charge of Venezuela" until the presidential elections. Faced with this situation, national and international personalities denounced that, according to the provisions of Article 233 of the Chavista constitution, it was not Maduro who should assume the charge, but Cabello. However, on March 8, 2013, the "Chavista" Constitutional Chamber of the TSJ decided that Maduro's oath of office as "president in charge" was appropriate. So, that before the decision of the Supreme Court, the opposition had to give in its "constitutional right" to place the "ultra" Chavista Diosdado Cabello in president.

CHAVEZ'S DEATH

On the death of Chávez, I had never seen so many stories, hypotheses, versions. There are those who persist that the date of his death is not the one that the government made known. In fact, in my opinion, Maduro, for security reasons of transfer of power, did not give a date, until he saw that he had everything under his control. So on March 5, 2013, on radio and television, confirmed the death of its revolutionary leader.

A few months before, on December 8, 2012, Chávez announced in Caracas that he is returning to Cuba to continue treatment for cancer, and urges the country, which, faced with its possible lack, "elect Nicolás Maduro as president."

In March 2012 he returned to Cuba again, and spent almost three months in the Center for Medical Surgical Research (CIMEQ) in Havana. From his stay there, he wanted to hide everything about his condition, or treatment. In fact, the government never got clear, what kind of cancer Chávez had, where in his body he is located, and how developed he was when he was detected.

Many people rumored that he had already died. After these rumors, the Venezuelan government on February 15, 2013, brought to light, about four photos, where Chávez was accompanied by his daughters, while he was bedridden. A lot of controversy occurred about those photos, since the president was seen holding a Cuban newspaper with a date on the cover, with the idea of proving himself, that he was still alive. There are those who have stated that the photos were faked, and that on the image of the newspaper, they placed another manipulated image, with a much later date.

In February 2013, without informing anyone of his travel plans, and in the middle of the night, Chavez returned to Venezuela, and was admitted to an army hospital in Caracas. From that return, there are no photos, videos, showing that after his arrival in the country, he was alive.

And how was it that people heard about his arrival? Well, it was by means of a very short written message, which supposedly he had hung on the networks, two hours after his arrival. On this fact, for some surprising, there is the antecedent, that, during the previous 69 days, Chávez did not make any public appearance, nor was evidence revealed about his health since his last operation in Havana.

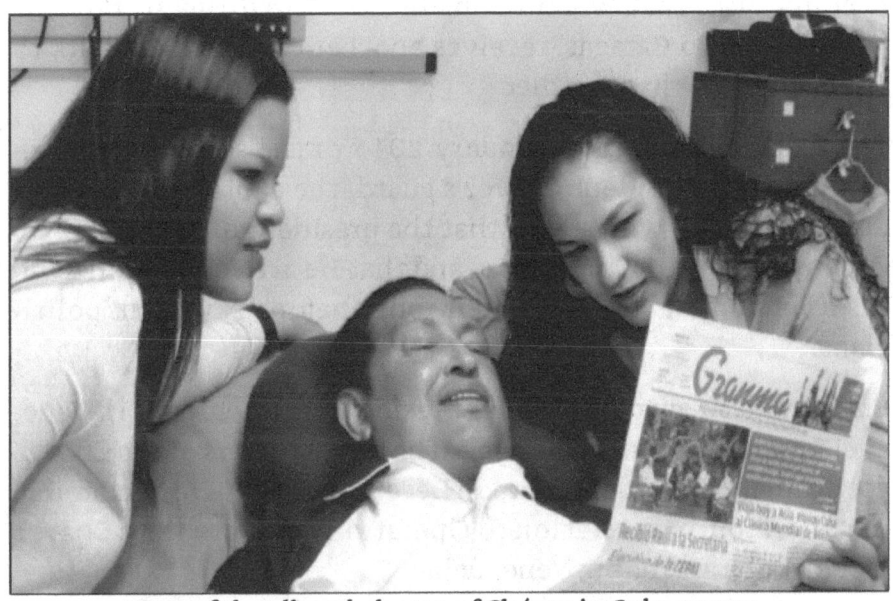

One of the alleged photos of Chávez in Cuba accompanied by his daughters.

Of that arrival, there are some anecdotes. For example, the main state channel, Venezolana de Televisión (VTV), broadcast a photograph in which it is seen going down a ladder of the presidential Airbus, in the company of two of his daughters, but the chain VTV later specified on its website, that it was a file image. Another news, and reported by the same television channel, presents the testimony of a nurse at the military hospital, who identified herself with credentials in hand as Dubraska Mora, who stated that the "commander" would not have entered the health center not only standing but "without any invasive process", suggesting with his words the remission of the tumor he Chávez suffered.

There are hypotheses that Chavez died in Havana before the officially announced date. In an interview, Attorney General Luisa Ortega Díaz said that on December 28, 2012, during a trip outside Venezuela, she received a call from Diosdado Cabello, asking her to return to the country, because Chávez had died. Account also, that when he made the formalities to buy the tickets back to Caracas, receives another call from Cabello, to tell him that he had not died.

There are statements in January 2015 of the second officer in command of President Chávez's guard, the captain of corvette Leamsy Salazar, who stated that the president died at 17:32 on December 30, 2012 in Havana, and that He arrived dead in Caracas, a version that had been mentioned before by various politicians.

Euzenando Azevedo, who was president of Odebrecht in Venezuela, and also a liaison between the top members of the Chávez government and Odebrecht, on December 16, 2016, declared in Brazilian courts in relation to Operation Lava Jato, that Chávez died in Cuba and not in Venezuela.

And to all this, there is a diversity of rumors. For example, they talk about coffin changes in their move to Caracas, and the possible use of a Chavez wax replica. To this, are added the statements of embalmers who traveled to Cuba, and alleged reactions of those who saw the face of the deceased president. Undoubtedly, all these "rumors" support the idea that everything has been a show mounted by the Government, or rather, by the same Nicolás Maduro. In fact, there are "supposed" photos of the corpse, which does not appreciate the much-questioned wart that Chávez had on the upper part of his face, with which, from there, to affirm that whoever was inside the coffin was a wax-work.

After knowing his death, the corpse was paraded through the streets of Caracas, in a kind of funeral procession. The "supposed" corpse, traveled inside a coffin. Later, in the Military Academy of Caracas, a funerary chapel was installed that lasted 10 days, where his corpse was exposed to the public in a glass case, so that anyone who wanted to visit, could give their respects. But only people could be at most, three seconds.

Later, on March 15, Chávez would be transferred to his mausoleum in the Cuartel de la Montaña de Caracas, and they would definitively seal his grave, with a black granite drawer.

During the exhibition of the body of Chávez, both in the funerary chapel of the Military Academy, and in the Cuartel de la Montaña, visitors had to leave out the cameras, recorders, mobile phones, and any device that could record images.

According to the government, about two million people saw the body. It is noteworthy that is that there are thousands of people, who say that what they saw was a wax figure, because the body had a smooth skin too bright and pink, her lips natural color closed, had some hair covered by a cap red and the neck also smooth and whole without the marks of the tracheotomy that the practiced him when he was convalescing in Cuba.

Many of the people who saw the wax figure, and had denounced it in the networks as a hoax, paid dearly for its audacity. This is the case of the tweeter Lourdes Ortega, who for saying in her account @ulilou "I do not know but turned into wax is", was arrested for 24 hours on orders of Maduro. The excuse for his arrest was because Ortega intended to "destabilize" Venezuela with those comments.

Mausoleum where today are the "alleged body" Chávez remains.

In short, for many, the truth is that Chávez they took him ill to Cuba, since for many "communists", Cuba is the miracle of medicine. And in the end, the president acquired a lung infection during his treatment in the so-called "medical paradise", which would lead to his death.

Before the death of the "commander", "Maduro", took place, an entire plan was set up with his official version of events, for him to be able to take over without problems, and without enemies in sight, the power inherited by Chavez himself, that he had chosen him as his successor. One wonders, what was the participation of the Cuban regime, since without doubt, Raúl Castro was interested in having his strong man (Maduro) defending the interests of Havana in Caracas.

And to end the issue, there are those who affirm that if instead of going to Cuba, Chávez had gone to Brazil, or Argentina, to get treatment, today the "commander" would still be alive.

THE ELECTORAL FRAUD OF 2013

Many had criticized the official date of death given by Maduro, as well as his temporary appointment as president in charge, with which, for many, especially for the opposition, the fact that Maduro called presidential elections on day 14 , did not have much of a certain legality .

For this call, almost 19 million people are called to the polls. They vote about 15 million, with a participation of 79%. And the expected result, is the victory of Maduro, by 50.61%, against his opponent, Henrique Capriles, who got the 49.12%. A result cataloged by many as of infarct !.

In the campaign of these elections, he highlighted the great inequality in terms of excessive government control over the media, giving a disproportionate amount of television space to Maduro, with practically no space for opposition. The government unleashed a genuine "negative campaign" against Capriles. For example, Maduro used comments that were considered homophobic, calling Capriles "little princess", and declaring during a massive campaign event that "I do have a wife, I like women", to which Capriles responded to it, rejecting the comments on his sexuality, describing himself as "single", and affirming that he had a progressive vision of life, condemning the homophobic stance of his opponent.

Capriles declined to sign a document of the National Electoral Council (NEC) committing to recognize the result, as he did before the elections on October 7, pledging instead to "respect the popular will." Diosdado Cabello, a Chavista leader, had presented a series of supposed evidences, with telephone recordings, emails and other documents, supposedly showing that the opposition planned not to recognize the electoral results.

The opposition leader Henrique Capriles.

On April 12, Vice President Jorge Arreaza announced on national television that the government had arrested two Colombians who had presented themselves as Venezuelan military officers and had tried to interrupt the elections. And additionally, Arreaza claimed that they located a cage of weapons, which is linked to Salvadoran mercenaries, which the government had previously accused, of conspiring to kill Maduro.

On the night of April 14, after knowing the results, Capriles ignored the official bulletin issued by the NEC, and called for a total count of the votes, since according to his campaign command, had detected at least 3500 alleged irregularities during the voting process. The international community, through the governments of Spain, France, the US, Paraguay, and the OAS Secretary General, José Miguel Insulza, joined to said complaints by the opposition

Maduro accepted the performance of the audit proposed by the opposition, but the NEC stated that in Venezuela the process was automated, and that the proposed audit could not be carried out in the proposed terms, since according to this organization, it was not provided for in the order legal. In other words, the Chavistas mounted an electoral system to suit them, where the opponent did not have the legal mechanisms to challenge an electoral process.

On April 17, Capriles submitted his application formally, with all the corresponding complaints and the request for the total verification of the minutes. The NEC met for hours that same day, until accepting the verification "in the second phase", of 46% of the non-audited voting urns at random at first. This audit however was not endorsed by Capriles, arguing that the same "should have been carried out together with a review of the voting papers", for which the process was challenged before the Supreme justice court (TSJ).

On June 11, 2013, the NEC announced the completion of the audit, supporting the victory of Maduro.

So one of the hopes that the opposition had, was to wait for the chavista TSJ will fix a position, which was known, on August 7, 2013, announcing that unanimously, they declared inadmissible all the impuctions to the results of the 14th April 2013.

And what other option was left to the opposition? On September 9, 2013, they presented the impugnment to the elections before the Inter-American Commission on Human Rights (CIDH). It was useless, since a day later, the Chavista government had formally abandoned that institution, in prediction, that if at some point the CIDH condemned Venezuela, then, as the country is no longer part, is not obliged to accept anything.

And while that panorama was developing with accusations of conspiracies and electoral fraud, the Venezuelan on foot, began to suffer with more rigor the scarcity of food, medicines, and insecurity in the streets. The increase in the murder rate was higher than ever, considering Caracas, the most violent city in the world.

THE COLOMBIAN ORIGIN OF MADURO

As for the legitimacy of Nicolás Maduro, as head of government, there is a very interesting story.

After assuming the presidency, the rumor spread that he was born in Colombia. In Venezuelan law, established that to be president, only citizens born in Venezuelan territory could apply. The issue is that all this erupted months after taking office, and of course, from there, much has been written about the origin of Nicolás Maduro.

It has been said that she was not born in a maternity, and that she was born in a private house, for which reason there are no records in the maternity wards of her birth. Representatives of the opposition have traveled to Colombia to investigate the past of the Maduro family. It is known with certainty that the father (Nicolás Maduro), the mother (Teresa de Jesús Moros Acevedo) and the sister of the president (María Teresa de Jesús Maduro Moros), are Colombians, and Maduro, being child, he lived and studied in Colombia.

On July 29, 2013, Guillermo Cochez, former ambassador of Panama to the Organization of American States (OAS), showed in the Colombian tv program NTN24 the birth certificate of the president, and it showed that Nicolás Maduro was born in the Colombian city of Cúcuta.

And Maduro, what did he say to all this?. For his part, nothing, but his high Chavistas comrades, have run various picturesque versions. In one of them, it is indicated, that the register where the birth appears, was burned, for which reason, there is no official document. It is also said that he was not born in a maternity, if not, in a private house in Caracas. The question is that there are those who give two different places of birth within Caracas. A mystery!

On October 10, 2013, the president of the NEC, Tibisay Lucena, showed, before the cameras of the news channel Globovisión, in Caracas, the "supposed" birth certificate of Maduro. Lucena had pointed out that in said birth certificate, belonging to La Candelaria Parish in Caracas, it is explained that Nicolás Maduro was given birth in a Caracas polyclinic. The funny thing is that what Lucena had presented before the television cameras, it was not a birth certificate, but a photocopy of a page of a book where the births are registered, where to top it off, the name of the supposed clinic is not specified. In short, with this new version, more new doubts were created.

But to top it off even more the situation of this history full of drama and suspense, at the end of January 2017, the Supreme Court of Venezuela (under Chavista control), he announced a resolution, which allows a Venezuelan president to have dual citizenship. So, with that, already the matter of the Colombian origin of Maduro, has been solved!

And to this day, Mr. Maduro has never shown his official birth document.

THE REPRESSION VERSION
NICOLÁS MADURO

In February 2014, Venezuela is once again on the front pages of all the media in the world. For many Venezuelans, on February 12, it is a symbolic date, as it commemorates the day of youth, in memory of José Félix Rivas, a patriot who fought alongside Simón Bolívar. Since January of that year, in the city of Mérida, student protests against the government were registered. In those days, was announced, the death of the student Héctor Moreno, of the Universidad de los Andes, at the hands of government forces.

The main objective of the protesters, was to get the resignation of Maduro, and with it, the change of the political-economic model of Venezuela. Many protesters considered the regime as a dictatorship inspired by the socialist state model, directed from Cuba.

By February 12, they are called by the opposition, and the student sector, various demonstrations in the major cities of the country. For its part, the response of the government was to call on counter-demonstrations in favor of Maduro, where the government's message or slogan is to define the opposition as "coup-makers" and "fascists".

So, in front of the many anti-Maduro student demonstrations in the cities of Mérida, San Cristóbal, or Caracas, the government's security forces applied violence as a response, as well as the arrest and imprisonment of student leaders. One of these imprisoned leaders is Leopoldo López, whom Maduro accused directly of being behind the organization of the demonstrations. Meanwhile, in those days, at least 28 people die in acts of violence.

Opposition demonstration of Caracas in February 2014.

Among the many "burradas" that Maduro said in those days, for example, had come to affirm that the city of San Cristóbal was besieged by "right-wing paramilitaries" under the orders of Colombian President Álvaro Uribe. Uribe, on the other hand, rejected these declarations saying that they were a tactic of distraction of Maduro before the real problems of the country, like inflation, or the insecurity in the streets. Maduro had also said that the opposition mayor of San Cristóbal, Daniel Ceballos, would soon join López "behind bars for fomenting violence." In the end, Ceballos was arrested in March by the Bolivarian National Intelligence Service (SEBIN) without an arrest warrant, and suspended and dismissed of his position as mayor by the TSJ for contempt of court, by order of the Public Ministry. Thus, a mayor of the opposition, who had won an election, was a victim of the Chavistas persecution. The same fate would run later, the opposition mayor of Caracas, Antonio Ledezma.

Another detail to highlight of those days, is the role of the so-called "collectives", basically groups of motorized, financed and armed by the same government, whose role is to put fear into the opposition in the streets. Already several Venezuelan human rights organizations had denounced that these groups receive weapons from the Venezuelan government, and that they have the mission of being "shock guards" of Chavismo.

According to the Colombian news channel NTN24, in March 2014, the Chavistas groups violently participated in 437 protests, approximately 31% of the total of the protests in March, where bullet wounded were reported. The armed groups have been accused of attacking and burning the Fermín Toro University, after intimidating the protesting students, and firing at one of them.

For its part, Amnesty International reported that in those days of February, they had received reports of the use by state security forces of "rubber bullets and tear gas fired directly at demonstrators at close range and without warning "and that" these practices violate international standards and have resulted in the death of at least one demonstrator. "

To all this, a report of the Venezuelan Criminal Forum is added, where it is indicated, that for those dates, there had been registered 18 cases of torture to detainees. These tortures, some by SEBIN, would include beatings, electric shocks, and asphyxiation, in addition to psychological torture. The detainees would be denied access to lawyers and would be forced to sign a document declaring that they had been served by defense lawyers.

In short, the response of the Chavismo to student demonstrations, was persecution, shooting, arbitrary detention, torture, and no right to have an adequate defense detainees. A, without forgetting that there are reports of rape against women, by armed government officials. And not only women. In those days, the case of Juan Manuel Carrasco was reported, beaten and sexually violated by officials of the Bolivarian National Guard (GNB), who according to forensic evidence made after the fact, corroborate the violation, denying the General Prosecutor of the Chavista government, which did not recognize the facts.

THE HUNGER BUSINESS IN VENE-
ZUELA, AS A WAY TO CONSOLIDATE
THE BOLIVARIAN REVOLUTION

Regarding the issue of the economy, in 2013, according to the figures of the Central Bank of Venezuela (BCV), the country recorded the highest inflation in the world, exceeding 50%. Companies like Toyota, closed their facilities, as well as many others, as is the case ofcompanys various pharmaceutical, food, agricultural, etc.

The reason for these closures, is thanks to the Chavista policy of destroying the productive apparatus of the country, with the sole purpose of confiscating all that, which the same regime, has led directly to bankruptcy. The ridiculous aspect of this policy of confiscation is that Maduro believes, or tries to make his followers understand, that confiscating something that has been ruined by the government itself can be profitable, and more so when it delivers the management of those companies, to people who do not have the slightest idea, to manage a company. And as it will be understood, the logical result in all this, is that the large amount of money that the government has invested to supposedly reactivate a bankrupt company, is more corruption and waste of money, while the ordinary people, every day passes more hunger, since the companies of the alimentary sector, have closed, or rather, have been forced to close before the terrible economic management of the state.

According to the Federation of Chambers of Commerce of Venezuela (Fedecámaras), in 2014, the debt in dollars of the government with the private sector of laboratories and the pharmaceutical industry, is of 2,300 million dollars. And as with that productive sector, it happens the same in all other sectors of the country.

In 2014, Venezuela suffered its highest food shortage in five years, with 26%. And Maduro's response to the problem is accusing various companies of hoarding food.

And for the few companies that remain in the country, the government does not give if a single dollar to import the inputs or machinery to produce. But on the other hand, there are some high government officials who, if they get dollars, to buy on behalf of the government, thousands of containers with expired or rotten foods to companies installed in countries allied to the regime, as is the case of Nicaragua. And for that, billions of dollars were distributed, which have served to increase corruption in the top Chavistas leaders.

Maduro opens the CLAP bag packaging center in March 2017.

For example, since 2016, the government distributes bags of basic foodstuffs to the population through a Local Supply and Production Committee (CLAP). These foods, the vast majority, are brought from outside the country, and paid with "preferential" dollars that the government gives to its "business" friends (military and chavistas) so that they can buy them by skipping all control, inspection, and health, and so bring those foods in containers to Venezuela. The people on foot who buy these imported products have to pay a price set by the government it-self. The issue is that the bag of imported food is usually distrib-uted to people once a month, although there are many people who take up to two months to see the bag.

And what products are inside that bag?. Depending on the exist-ence in stock. Sometimes a liter of oil, a packet of rice, a packet of pasta, 1 kilo of milk powder, or a kilo of cornmeal.

In September of 2017, a product bag CLAP had a public price of about 10 thousand Bolívares fuertes (Bfs). It is worth noting that with the exchange control system that was in effect for that date in the country by the same government, the price of the currency for the purchase of food at a preferential rate was 10 Bfs to the dollar, which reveals the incredible level of cor-ruption of the CLAP. To have an idea, a box or bag of products, for the government, costs about 20 US dollars. When dealing with food, the same government, sets an exchange rate of 10 Bfs, per dollar, with which, the real price of each bag or box, is about 200 Bfs. And in the end, the government sells it to people in 10,000 Bfs. Now, multiply this profit by thousands and thou-sands of bags that have sold in a rationalized way, and to top it all, with expired or adulterated products. In short, the same government, through the CLAP, have set up a very, very, very lucrative business, where some are filled with dollars when im-porting expired products with over-priced invoices, and others are filled with Bfs, with a super speculation of the sale of expired products to the Venezuelan citizen of the street.

The so-called CLAPs are made up of representatives of the councils, in addition to the National Union of Women, and the so-called Bolívar-Chávez Battle Fronts. That is, it is a 100% Chavista organization, whose mission is to make a census of those who have the right to buy that bag of food. If there is someone who speaks ill of Maduro or the "revolution", That per-son has no right to buy your bag of food. And the worst of all, is that nobody controls how the distribution of these foods is made. In fact, there are managers of those CLAP who steal food shipments, to do business in the black market, or go to the so-called "bachaqueros", which are street vendors, who offer these foods at more than double the price fixed by the CLAP.

One of the many protests about the poor distribution of CLAP bags in Caracas. Not all bags reach their recipients.

And where do the food come from ?. Well, the Maduro government has given millions of dollars to their friends, so they can set up the business of their lives, bringing food from countries like Ecuador, Nicaragua or Mexico, to Venezuela. These are brought in containers in various vessels, which arrive at various ports in the country, and there, they are unloaded, and distributed to the CLAP. The problem is that this distribution is usually not very clear, and in the end, much of the merchandise is lost along the way, and it ends up in the hands of the "speculators" friends of the "revolution". It has also been the case, that some containers, are forgotten, and food simply rot. Or it has also been the case, that other foods, after their arrival in the cities, have discovered that the expiration date expired, and have opted to over mark the dates, and pass them as healthy foods for human consumption, and all this without going through any type of sanitary control on the part of the Venezuelan authorities. And if you think, what I said is little ... well ... here I tell you an anecdote: In 2018, an old lady, known to my family, after doing a few walks, she was able to get some tuna cans who sold him the so-called "bachaqueros". After arriving home, he saw that in the cans, they had their label with the name of the manufacturer, and saw that the product had been manufactured in Ecuador. But he could not see any expiration date, since it had been erased. When opening the first can, he found the surprise, that along with the tuna, there was an insect, whence, the poor woman opted not to consume the product. And this example of the tuna can, happens with the rest of the food.

Another example is that the government brings milk powder from Mexico, and that milk does not have the minimum quality necessary for human consumption. A laboratory of the Central University of Venezuela (UCV), in 2018, made an analysis of several brands of milk brought from Mexico. According to the world health organization, a child, for its training and development, needs at least one glass of milk per day, with which, it would provide the necessary calcium. Well, in that laboratory of the UCV, after the analysis, they came to the conclusion that for a Venezuelan child to have the necessary calcium levels, he would have to take more than 100 glasses of that Mexican milk. And all thanks to who ?. Well, thanks to the dollars that the government of Maduro gave to a "businessman" Chavista, who filled his pockets with one of the many scams that have been mounted, playing with the hunger and misery of the Venezuelan people, on behalf of the "Bolivarian revolution". Today, Venezuela has the highest rates of malnutrition in its history. And the unfortunate thing is that there are older people and children, who die because of it, while the government continues in its campaign that the fault of the shortage is the "fascist businessmen", or the "bachaqueros", who They sell expired products brought in containers from abroad by the same government.

Thousands of Venezuelans every day look for food in the trash.

It seems that one of the strategies used by Chavismo, to perpetuate itself in power, is to make the people go hungry and misery, in order to control the people. In Cuba, the people of that country, since the arrival of the communist revolution, live depending on ration cards for basic products (soap, clothes, etc.) and food (rice, meat, pulses, etc.). The Cuban government is the one that establishes, what amount of rice, or meat, every Cuban has the right to eat during a month, or how many shirts, or shoes, can be bought during a year. So, the population of that country, depends their life, of ration cards, while the communist regime tells them for 50 years, that they go hungry, because of the blockade of the US. Thus, Cubans have become accustomed to the idea that their government helps them to survive in the face of the demonized "American blockade", while in the five-star hotels of the island, tourists live in luxury, eating of everything without using a ration card. So, the Cuban of the street, going hungry, feels grateful, because the "revolutionary" government gives them the supposed right to go hungry.

In the case of Venezuela, there is only the difference that Chavismo does not give ration cards, since with that, it would be forced to feed, well, if it can be called that, feed the population. So, what the Venezuelan government has invented, is a kind of "ration cards" called the fatherland card. Without that card, you do not have the right to buy the bag of expired products distributed arbitrarily by the CLAP. By the way, the excuse used by the Venezuelan government to justify that people go hungry, is the so-called "economic war." In short, a Venezuelan happens the double or triple the hunger than a Cuban.

And not only the famine is killing the lives of Venezuelans. Added to this is the dramatic increase in violence on the streets. For 2013, the Venezuelan Observatory of Violence had affirmed that in Caracas there are 79 deaths per 100 thousand inhabitants, almost 25 thousand Venezuelans killed by violence in a year, while the Ministry of the Interior only recognizes 39 per 100 thousand inhabitants. According to the same Observatory, for the year 2016 this figure rose to 91.8 homicides per 100 thousand inhabitants. In contrast, the prosecution recognizes 70.1 per 100 thousand inhabitants, which represents 8 times more than the global average. So, we find ourselves with the dramatic paradox, that if in Venezuela they do not kill you to take off a pair of shoes, you die of hunger, malnutrition, or thanks to a disease like dengue.

And what have the Venezuelans done to express their discontent in this situation? After diversity of marches, demonstrations, general strikes ... only the Venezuelan of the street, has used the calls barricades, popularly known in Venezuela with the name of "guarimbas". But what good is it to stop or close an avenue, or a street, if in the end, Maduro, does not go to the avenues or a streets where protests take place. In addition, the so-called "guarimberos", only have stones and sticks, to face tanks and machine guns of the government police forces. And in this, in the case of a possible confrontation, Maduro has all the advantages of having at his disposal the power to use the full force of a dictatorial system of oppression.

So, in 2018, we find that more than 2 million Venezuelans, in less than a year, have left the country, tired of fighting, and hopefully, both the government and the opposition, take on the challenges to rebuild a country. Not only the government is the big responsible. The political opposition also has its great share of responsibility, for not knowing how to use the appropriate mechanisms to get the Chavistas out of power.

THE ANTONIO LEDEZMA CASE

Antonio Ledezma, days before being arrested.

In February 2015, the Maduro government accused the opposition mayor of Caracas, Antonio Ledezma, of planning a coup with the support of the US. On the 19th, he was arrested in his office by a SEBIN commando. The images of his detention were seen all over the world, thanks to the recordings of the surveillance cameras of the building where the raid took place. In short, another opposition mayor, in full exercise of his office, is arrested by the government. On the night of the same day, Maduro revealed that by order of the Attorney General, Ledezma is accused of being a participant in the so-called "Operation Jericho", which sought to overthrow the government, being, according to complaints of the opposition, this the "twelfth attempt of coup d'état "that the president denounces. After passing Ledezma held in a military prison, and then, imprisoned in his own home, on November 17, 2017, he flees from Venezuela, having spent 1002 days of detention.

As for how Ledezma left the country, it is not very clear. He gave a version, for me, something not credible, where he indicated, that in his escape by road, traveled 840 kilometers from Caracas to the border with Colombia, passing through more than 20 roadblocks, and helped by some Venezuelan military. But one thing if I can assure. For him to arrive in Cucuta, Colombia, with a Venezuelan passport, he did not do it alone. I think that someone, from the same government of Maduro, put the escape plan in motion. Perhaps they planned everything up, with the idea of stopping it in the middle of the border, and thus, telling the world, that they arrested a dangerous conspirator. But as the government does all the wrong things, but very badly, the plan to stop a "terrorist" in escape, it got out of hand, and by some chance of fate, Ledezma was able to escape. Another thing that has caught my attention about this leak is how Ledezma was able to achieve something so difficult to obtain, as is the passport. As I have said before, since 2017 the government does not provide passports, which is a luxury item that is difficult to obtain. I insist, in principle, it would be even more difficult to obtain, if the owner is imprisoned in his house for being an enemy of the government. In fact, and I am sure, the first thing that the government did when they detained him for the first time in 2015, was to take away and cancel his passport. One more case of the very rare things that happen in the country.

THE VICTORY OF THE OPPOSITION AND THE CREATION OF A CHAVISTA PARALLEL PARLIAMENT

On December 6, 2015, elections are held to elect the Parliament. After 16 years of control of the Chavistas in the National Assembly, and despite the fact that they continued to use the same electoral method with the "machines", in the end, the opposition won 112 seats, compared to 55 for the government. That is, with the same system of fraud always used by the government, the Chavistas could not minimize their electoral failure, despite the fact that, as in the previous campaigns, the Chavista government used all the resources of the same State, to Campaign for their candidates.

Meeting of the new opposition parliament in the congress of Venezuela.

Moreover, one of the tactics used by the regime to intimidate the opposition and do the most damage to it was the political disqualification of several opposition leaders who wanted to participate in the December 6 elections. Among the disqualified by the Chavista justice were Manuel Rosales, Pablo Perez, Maria Corina Machado, Daniel Ceballos, Enzo Scarano, Carlos Vecchio and Leopoldo Lopez, who already had a previous disqualification, and which was ratified until 2017. This was denounced by the Organization of States Americans (OAS) as disqualifications that "only operate for opposition leaders" in "prejudiced cases" based on unsubstantiated accusations.

After knowing the official results, Maduro denounced an alleged fraud that the opposition would have committed by means of a supposed "vote buying" by opposition candidates to guarantee votes in their favor. Maduro claimed to have proof, and had entrusted the investigation to the Chavista mayor of the Libertador municipality of Caracas, and head of the government campaign command, Jorge Rodríguez. Subsequently, Rodríguez made a public address where he claimed to have gathered testimony and evidence of the occurrence of irregularities that vitiated the effects of the election, specifically in the state of Amazonas, and had urged the NEC to investigate such alleged events.

In short ... the same chavista government who created, developed, and controlled the electoral process, now leaves with the story that there is a fraud, and that the result of the elections should be annulled in those regions of the country where the Chavistas were defeated.

Additionally, Maduro publicly denounced as an alleged "irregular" situation the abundance of invalid votes registered in the elections, assuring that the sum of them equaled "one and a half million votes". Maduro insisted that such not chavistas votes, presumably are the result of deliberate bad advice from polling station members to voters, had succeeded in altering the results in specific circuits. He presented as an example the electoral circuit number 3 of the state Aragua, where the opposition candidate got his seat with only 82 votes of difference of the official candidate.

For electoral experts, the null votes could not be argued as nullity effects for the national election, firstly, because the null vote is not a cause for objection. Likewise, the number of null votes denounced by the president Maduro was oversized, and according to comparative analyzes of the 2015 election with other precedents, they did not represent a significant increase to be considered an irregularity. According to the individual analysis of the electoral circuits nationwide, the cases in which a candidate won with a greater number of null votes than the rival candidate were greater in favor of the ruling party than the opposition.

Weeks after the elections, the opposition denounced that the TSJ wanted to impugn the electoral process in a number of districts that affected some 22 elected deputies, and that additionally, they wanted to prevent the swearing in of said deputies. Before said complaint, the TSJ denied said information. But yes, a week later, the TSJ officially announced that it had accepted 7 complaints of impugns that affected a total of 8 deputies elected to represent the states of Amazonas, Aragua and Yaracuy.
At the end of this plot, in January 2016, three opposition deputies renounce the National Assembly under pressure from the TSJ, leaving the opposition coalition, without the majority needed to block the laws proposed by Maduro.

And although Maduro, to some extent, achieved the impossible in front of the opposition Parliament, he, later, will opt for a new tactic: Create a Chavista Parliament parallel to his measure, with the intention of delegitimizing the majority-elected Parliament opposing, and for that, he announces that for the month of July of 2017, a Constituent Assembly will be elected, with which, the regulation establishes, that for this purpose, the newly elected Parliament should be dissolved in December, and of course, with that, Maduro would have the opportunity to try to mount another Parliament, designed by him, and without opposition leaders. That is, it will create a parallel "illegal" Parliament, with 100% of Chavistas leaders.

In front of this announcement of the convocation of the constituent Assembly, in September 2016, thousands of people protest in Caracas demanding the resignation of Maduro. But despite the protests, Maduro remains in power, as if nothing.

Between the months of April and July of 2017, a wave of protests is developing at the National level, with a tragic balance of more than 90 people dead. The protesters demanded advanced presidential elections, and the suspension of the Constituent Assembly. Maduro's response was to order public employees to vote for the Constituent Assembly. The chavista government slogan was: public employee who does not vote for the government, employee fired from office.

Today, Venezuela has more than 2.8 million public employees, which means that Maduro has 2.8 million votes secured. And you will wonder why the country has the highest rate of public employees in the world ?. Well, very simple. The more employees you have, the more votes in your favor. To give you an idea that this is a Chavismo strategy, I am going to give you a dat:

Since 1999, when the "commander" came to power, until 2015, the number of employees in the country increased by more than 100%! That is to say, the country with the Chavismo has more than double the number of employees, and with that, I insist, haven a direct guarantee of almost 3 million votes. Thus, it is understood to some extent, as money is squandered in the country.

By the way, I remembered an anecdote about public officials in Venezuela. In 1999, after the arrival of the revolution, in a Venezuelan university, we wanted to make a study on why the racecourse in Caracas, was the only racetrack in the world, which produced losses, despite, supposedly, every weekend , millions and millions of bolivares, were collected in bets. So they looked at figures of the staff that works there, and for example, they saw that for the cleaning service, they had hired about 180 people. After doing a study on the real needs of personnel, they deduced, that with 35 people, it gave more than enough to keep the facilities clean. That is to say, more than 140 people had been hired for this clean-up job. And if we see that this happens with the other jobs such as secretaries, security guards, etc., it could be perfectly understood, because it is the only racecourse in the world that has mony lost. And the example of the hippo-drome of Caracas, can be transferred to the rest of the State institutions, and thus, we understand, because Venezuela has more than 2.8 million public officials. Another fact: Venezuela is the country with the highest positions of ministers in the world with 34! (data of 2018) To give an idea with other coun-tries, for example, in Germany, that there is more than twice the population that in Venezuela, in that country, there are barely 14 ministries. In short, the Chavism has created a political sys-tem, with which having 34 ministries, that it gives to create much more corruption, and, on the other hand, with it buy the votes of 2.8 million people (public workers).

On July 30, 2017, elections were held to choose the 545 mem-bers of the Constituent Assembly, and on August 4 it was for-mally installed in the Elliptical Hall of the Federal Legislative Palace (also the seat of the National Assembly). The striking thing about this "Assembly" is that everyone, I insist, all its members are Chavistas. Supposedly, the idea of said Assembly, was to write a new constitution, for which, a period of two years was fixed. An important detail in all this story of the "Constituent Assembly", is that the chavista TSJ, dictates the decision 156. by means of which, said "Constituent Assembly" attributes to itself the functions of the National Assembly, and extends the powers of President Maduro, according to the Con-stitutional Chamber "until the situation of contempt persists" of Parliament. That is to say, at that moment, in Venezuela there are two Parliaments. One elected with an opposition majority despite the chavism traps, whose resolutions are ignored by the regime; and another Parliament assembled by Maduro, with 100% Chavista members, whose illegal decisions have to be followed at gunpoint.

Installation day of the Chavista Constituent Assembly.

And what have been the great achievements of the new "Chavista National Constituent Assembly" ?:

On August 5, 2017, the dismissal of Attorney General Luisa Ortega Díaz, who was previously suspended by the TSJ, is decided. Given the dismissal, the National Guard prevented Ortega from entering his workplace.

On August 16, 2017, Germán Ferrer, a Chavista deputy and husband of Attorney General Ortega, was removed the parliamentary immunity.

On October 26, 2017, dismisses Isaías Rodríguez, who until then had the position of second vice president in the Chavista Assembly. This happened after Rodriguez gave statements in the middle of an interview broadcast by the Venezuelan News Agency (AVN), where he acknowledged that the organism of which he was a part did not represent the solution to the social, economic and political problems suffered the country.

On November 6, 2017, authorizes the prosecution of the opposition deputy and first vice president of the National Assembly Freddy Guevara, a refugee in the Chilean embassy in Caracas, after the TSJ asked the organ to lift the parliamentary immunity.

On November 8, 2017, they approved a "law against hate". It establishes penalties of 20 years in prison, closure of media, and fines for companies and electronic media, among other sanctions. The law is controversial, and has been criticized in Venezuela by various sectors of society. And in spite of the criticism both inside and outside of Venezuela,s, it is still in full force.

On August 7, 2018, parliamentarian Juan Requesens was accused, along with also deputy and former president of the National Assembly Julio Borges, both leaders of the opposition, of being allegedly involved in the famous drone attack against Nicolás Maduro. The following day, the General Prosecutor's Office asked the TSJ to issue a ruling to allow the removal of the parliamentary immunity of Requesens and Borges, which was carried out and sent to the National Constituent Assembly, who approved it.

Finally, I have given a small sample of what the National Constituent Assembly has been, which has usurped the functions of Parliament, with violation of all national and international regulations, and has assumed full powers of the Venezuelan Parliament. And by the way, the gloomy thing about this whole story is that the authentic Parliament has been left in the background, and its decisions and resolutions are ignored by the chavista regime.

And if someone still asks, if the Constituent Assembly is legitimate, well, here is one piece of information:

Maduro, was the one who decided to create it, and according to article 348 of the Chavista Constitution, the president has only one role to propose it. And in the end, the town, with a consultation or referendum, is the one who decides, whether or not, convene and create such Assembly. This was what happened with the previous 1999 Assembly call.

But to remove doubts to the vices of illegality, everything in Venezuela, in the end is resolved, with a decision of the TSJ, which has a peculiarity, due to the fact that all its members were handpicked by the Chavistas. On June 7, 2017, the Constitutional Chamber of the TSJ, dictated sentence 378, where it decided that the president is entitled to convene a constituent without prior consultative referendum, since he acted in the name of the sovereignty of the people. In short, Maduro has more powers than his predecessor Chávez.

Another detail of the history: The only theoretical role that a National Constituent Assembly has, is to work on the drafting of a new constitution project, so that later, in a referendum, it is approved, or rejected by the population. The issue is that since it was installed, its only work has been to issue unconstitutional laws, agree to prosecute opposition leaders, or dismiss senior state officials who are questioned for their loyalty to the regime. In short, the Assembly has assumed the role of an "inquisitor tribunal".

Finally, I would like to make a kind of reflection with the case of the opposition deputy Julio Borges. Before his imminent imprisonment, Borges escaped to Colombia. On October 11, 2018, the Colombian government grants Borges refugee status. In short, another leader of the opposition who will no longer be able to set foot in Venezuela.

But unfortunately, all the opposition leaders have not had the same fate as Borges or Ledezma. Six days before, on October 5, the opposition councilor Fernando Albán, arrived from New York, after denouncing the Chavista regime at the UN headquarters. As soon as he stepped on the ground at the Maiquetía airport in Caracas, he was arrested on charges of having participated in the successful drones attack against Maduro. He was transferred to the headquarters of SEBIN, and according to the official version of the government, the detainee requested to go to the bathroom on the 10th floor of SEBIN's headquarters, and then, he threw himself from a window of said bathroom. So, the official version of the government is that the councilman committed suicide. After the denunciations of the opposition, where they emphasize that the detainee was tortured and murdered, almost nobody believes the version of suicide, and more when there are contradictions in the official version of the government.

Opposition Deputy Julio Borges.

Some people say that there are no windows in the bathrooms on the 10th floor of SEBIN. Given this fact, the Attorney General of Venezuela, the chavista Tarek William Saab, presented a photo at a press conference, which shows the image of a window in a hall of the building. Saab claimed that the photo corresponds to the place where the councilman was launched. The issue is that with this photo, the first official version is contradicted, since that photo is not from the interior of the bathroom where the detainee had initially been thrown. Moreover, they can not present the photo of the bathroom window, since there is no window.

The opposition councilor Fernando Albán.

Finally, faced with the obvious fact that the government itself does not know how to sustain its contradictory versions of what actually happened, they decide to go further by inventing another story with more than gloomy overtones. On October 12, the day the councilor was buried, the Chavista government says they have discovered that on the telephone of Councilman Albán, there were more than 2000 supposedly pornographic and pedophile videos, and that possibly, because of this, committed suicide. The Chavista government after killing him, they seek to discredit him, accusing him of being a pedophile, or mentally unbalanced. And the worst part of this story is that there will be someone from the chavista government who will say that the person who threw the councilor through the window of a 10th floor, did it for justice.

The fact is that in a short time, at the headquarters of SEBIN, two other detainees have died. One is Rodolfo Pedro González Martínez, who had been detained for more than a year for having participated in anti-Chavez demonstrations, and who supposedly, according to the official version of the government, in March 2015, committed suicide. And the other case is that of Councilman Carlos Andrés García, who died on September 17, 2017, after he was transferred from SEBIN to a hospital.

In short, three cases that have the common denominator that all are opponents, and all died in government custody.

And we must not forget, that according to the Venezuelan Criminal Forum, until October 2018, only in Caracas, there were more than 250 opposition political prisoners, in the custody of the government, and that they are in subhuman conditions because they do not have the basic rights to adequate attention to their cases. Many of the detainees suffer physical and psychological torture, and to this, it must be added that, being imprisoned in deplorable conditions in unhealthy places, over time they have acquired diseases, thanks in large part to the fact that they are poorly nourished. By the way, the death of Councilman Carlos Andrés García, was thanks to that. That is, he died after suffering a badly treated illness, or rather, for lack of medical attention in prison, and when they saw that death was imminent, they take him to a hospital, and then say, that the councilman did not die under in custody of the chavista government in jail.

THE ELECTORAL SUPER FRAUD
OF MADURO IN 2018

On March 1, 2018, the presidential elections were called, and in principle, the opposition had decided to participate in said elections. That is to say, I do not understand, as it is possible, that seeing what had happened in less than a year, with the illegitimate election of a Constituent Assembly, the opposition raises doubts about participating or not, in new elections, in which they already knew in advance, that they were going to be manipulated. I insist ... I do not understand, that before the various irregularities denounced during the convocation and the electoral process, including the political disqualification by judicial means, the impediment of participation of opposition parties, the lack of constitutional powers of the Constituent Assembly to call elections, the lack of time for the lapses established in the electoral regulations, and the purchase of votes, I insist, I do not understand how the leaders of the opposition, haven doubts to participate, or not, in new elections.

After the convocation illegal of the elections by the National Constituent Assembly, through an "unconstitutional" decree, some opposition parties fell into the game, by requesting a month-long postponement of the elections. That is to say, the political opposition goes to the alleged illegitimate Assembly, when recognizing its competences in setting up unconstitutional elections. In short, the opposition recognized on the one hand the legitimacy of something, which they say is illegal.

On March 1, 2018, a sector of the opposition, together with the Chavistas, signed an agreement to postpone the elections to May 20, and additionally, they agreed that international observers would participate in the process. I insist ... the opposition gentlemen, sign a paper, recognizing the "illegal" convocation of an election.

In the month of March 2018, the company Smartmatic, the company that throughout the chavism, set up the voting system with electronic electoral machines, announced its cessation of operations in Venezuela, stating that they could not guarantee the validity of the electoral results through your machines. So, if the same company that had parcipated in mounting the previous electoral frauds, did not guarantee the results of another fraud, I do not understand, as the opposition, I still wanted to participate in those new elections.

Well, one thing must be clear. In the end, a part of the Democratic Unity Table (MUD), which grouped the opposition parties, did not participate in the elections. Perhaps the fact that on January 25, 2018, the Constitutional Chamber of the TSJ, ordered the NEC to exclude the MUD from the process of validating ballots, making it impossible to participate in the presidential election, would have something to do with it. Tania D 'Amelio, one of the directors of the NEC, had declared that the MUD could not participate in the process because it had open judicial procedures in seven states. The same month, the main parties of the MUD (AD, Voluntad Popular and Avanzada Progresista), as well as spokespersons for the same, had announced that they would participate in the presidential elections. That same month, Juan Pablo Guanipa, Andrés Velásquez, Claudio Fermín, Henry Ramos Allup and Henri Falcón, announced their candidacies calling for a primary process within the MUD to elect the candidate for president for that coalition of parties.

And I insist ... with all that has happened, the opposition insisted on participating in another electoral fraud ?.

Finally, on February 21, the coalition parties, except Avanzada Progresista, reached an agreement not to participate in the elections. In a statement, the leaders of the MUD, had indicated that "The premature and unconditional event that is announced for next April 22 is only a show of the government itself to pretend a legitimacy that it does not have".

So, Maduro competed against only three candidates. One was Henri Falcón, of Avanzada Progresista, another was Javier Bertucci, for the party called El Cambio, and the third was the Chavista Reinaldo Quijada.

In the case of Falcón, after knowing his application, he was expelled from the MUD.

With 12 days to go before the elections, the NGO Observatorio Electoral Venezolano (OEV) published a 50-page document denouncing irregularities in the electoral process. For example, they indicated that there was disqualification of candidates, as well as the illegalization of political parties such as Primero Justicia, Puente, Voluntad Popular, and the most voted electoral card in the history of elections in Venezuela, that of the MUD. This report highlighted that one of the most serious consequences of a process with so many vices was "the devaluation (...) of the vote as a democratic way to resolve (...) differences and face the economic and social political crisis that the country is experiencing." Also in that report, it was pointed out that there is an indiscriminate use of public resources before the start and during the campaign by Maduro, as well as the use of the Fatherland Card , as a "coercion device", and as a stimulus for those who vote for the government. That is, that those people who present the card on the day of the elections, the government would give them money in exchange for their vote. To all this, the denunciations of the candidates of the opposition, by the limitation in the access to the means of communication, and the advantageism on the part of Maduro, when using resources and money of the state to finance their campaign are added.

So that you have an idea of how the Maduro government used all the resources of the State, to finance and develop its electoral campaign, I will quote an accusation from the Venezuelan newspaper Tal Cual Digital, who denounced in an article, how was the Maduro electoral campaign close. According to the newspaper, the act of closing the campaign on May 17 was "the greatest demonstration of corruption", criticizing the "brazen" use of public resources, including personnel structures of ministries. Said newspaper, published as evidence, an audio, which shows that the call was made using the payroll of government offices. Tal Cual also published the operational plan for the closure of the campaign of the United Socialist Party of Venezuela (PSUV), where it is appreciated that in the document the boxes corresponding to the responsible supporters appear empty, and responsibilities are directly assigned to the different ministries. public institutions, including the mobilization of groups of people. The operating plan described that PDVSA installed the main platform, power plants, backing and sound systems; that the Ministry of Defense was in charge of the detonations of fireworks; that the Ministry for Mining Development was responsible for the decoration; and that other offices were responsible for the installation of bathrooms, screens, barriers, awnings and refreshments. On page 6 of this document, it is also explained that on thea people group who they would go to the demonstration in the platform zone where Maduro it, there would plainclothes militiamen. In short ... a small sample of the "impartiality" of Maduro.

For the day of the elections, more than 20 million people are summoned, of which, according to the government, some 9 million vote, and according to the opposition, just over 3 million, with which, there is a "slight" difference of 5 million. In any case, if we pay attention to the government, the participation was 46%, being the lowest in the history of the country. And to top it off, the result was the triumph of Maduro, with 67% of the votes. That is, the same government recognizes that Maduro was elected president with just over 17% of the citizens called to vote.

And what have the opposition candidates said about all this? Well, to assume the same discourse of the past, that is to say, that the entire electoral process was a fraud, and that they would not recognize the results. Let's see if I understand: After everything seen, the background, the irregularities of the government, is there someone from the opposition, who believed, that Maduro was not going to manipulate the results?

Opposition leaders announce that they do not recognize the election result.

Finally, in spite of the rain of denunciations by the opposition, NGOs, and experts in electoral matters; and that more than a hundred governments did not recognize the results, on May 24, 2018, Maduro self-appointed as president before the 100% Chavista National Constituent Assembly, holding a ceremony, which should have taken place in January 2019, and before the National Assembly as ordered by article 231 of the Venezuelan Constitution. In view of this unconstitutional irregularity, the National Assembly with an opposition majority approved an agreement in which disown the electoral results and the re-election of Maduro, who "must be considered a usurper". And Maduro who has said all this? Well, tirili ... tirili ... he does not care.

By the way, at the end of September 2018, Maduro went to the UN Assembly to give his speech as president of Venezuela. Many of the countries that form the UN, months before, did not recognize him as president-elect. And I wonder ... if most of the UN countries do not recognize him as president of Venezuela, why did they invite him and allow him to give his speech?

At the end of 2018, several countries, as well as international organizations, such as the OAS or the EU, expressed their doubts about the legitimacy of Maduro as president. For example, the Minister of Foreign Affairs of Spain had come to say that they would wait until January 10, 2019, the "official" day of the end of Maduro's term, for Spain to establish a position. Likewise, the opposition in Venezuela raised the idea of waiting until January 10, although they announced, in view of Maduro's illegitimacy, the constitutional possibility that the president of the National Assembly (Parliament with a majority of opposition) could temporarily assume the presidency of the country, to convene in a few months a new clean elections.

Before this environment of illegitimacy that surrounded Maduro, it occurred to him that on January 10, he would swear again his position before the TSJ, an organ that is characterized by the fact, that the absolute majority of the judges that make it up , are some Chavistas handpicked by Maduro himself. So, Maduro organized a new show to justify his "legality" as president. In a chapter later, I'll tell you a little more about this story, and how this mess ended, or rather, how it got worse.

And something else ... Along with the presidential elections of 2018, elections were held of the legislative councils. And what do you think the result was? The party of Maduro, the PSUV, razed in all regions of the country.

THE FATHERLAND CARD

Along with the electoral system with voting machines that Chavismo created, another mechanism has been added to it that is almost as perfect, which undoubtedly makes it impossible for Maduro and the Chavistas to lose an election. We could say that it is an element of citizen control, created by the Maduro regime, and that consists of the so-called "fatherland card".

In December 2016, Maduro formally announced it, announcing that thanks to an agreement with China, that country would be responsible for the technological platform that would manage the control and issuance of said card. That is, the control of identity documents and passports, is in the hands of Cubans, and now, creates a new document, in quotation marks, not mandatory use, but under Chinese control.

The issue is that despite its supposed non-obligation to people to take it out, from the first moment, Maduro had already announced that whoever does not have such a card, will not be entitled to the benefits that the government supposedly gives, as it is the case of CLAP expired food bags, or being poorly served by Cuban doctors. Moreover, in 2018 the Chavista government stated that those retired people who do not have the said card, could not collect their pension of two dollars a month. So, that my mother, at 81, and against her will, was one of the many thousands of people who had to let herself be subjugated by the regime.

Faced with this threat environment, many Venezuelans, at the beginning, refused to take out the fatherland card, since they did not want to be identified with the Chavista regime. In fact, the idea of the card, is for the purpose, that its carrier, in some measure, keep loyalty to the regime. On the other hand, if that carrier does not show his loyalty to Maduro, he loses the card, and with all this, all the supposed benefits, or rights as a Venezuelan citizen.

According to government figures, by May 2017, more than thirteen million people had processed the card, assigning more than 200 thousand cards from the Mission Homes of the Nation, and at least 50 thousand student scholarships. That is, if a Venezuelan wishes to acquire a home, or a student scholarship, or his pension, if he does not have the "Chavista" card, he has no right.

It has reached the extreme, that in August 2018, Maduro announced that the price of gasoline would be sold in Venezuela at an international price, and that the one with the card could enjoy the old frozen price for 20 years. To get an idea of the frozen price, in 2018, with about 0.000050 cents of dolar, you can fill a tank of the car. Yes !, with about 0.000050 cents !. So that they have another idea of the gasoline business: With 1 dolar, in Venezuela it gives to fill the tanks of more than 1000 medium vehicles. Now, if a person do not have the card, the filling of the tank of the car, it would cost about 40 Euros, while the average salary in the country is about 2 Euros per month. Before this type of "blackmail", millions of Venezuelans, have been forced to get the card. By the way, in August 2018, I saw on TV, some images of Maduro in one of his chains, saying with a mocking spirit, that he already knew more than one opposition leader, who had his fatherland card. That is, without knowing it, he hinted, that he had his list of political opponents who have a fatherland card. And where do you think Maduro got the list from? Well, from your Chinese friends, whom the government has hired, for the management of the manufacturing of the cards.

Different sectors of society, opposition parties, unions, etc., have denounced this new form of government control. Venezuelan writer and journalist Leonardo Padrón, described the card as a "hunger-for-votes exchange". And you will wonder, how is that? Well, very simple:

Since the creation of this card, several electoral processes have been lived in Venezuela. During the development of electoral campaigns for these processes, the government encouraged the population, on the day of the vote, had to go to the polling place, presenting the card at the polling station, instead of the official identification document (identity card). In fact, there is an anecdote that I saw on television, that caused me, more laughter, than astonishment. During the elections of the National Constituent Assembly of 2017, the national television network Venezolana de Televisión, broadcast live and direct, when Maduro went to vote, and at the time of scanning his fatherland card to verify that he voted, everyone, On the television network, live and direct, he could clearly see that on the screen of the reader of the recording device he showed the message: "The person does not exist or the card was canceled". This I saw on TV, and millions of people saw it too. And before that overwhelming evidence of fraud, there are still those who believe that Maduro is a legitimate president ?. And to think that the Chinese charged millions of dollars, to ridicule Maduro with his fatherland card.

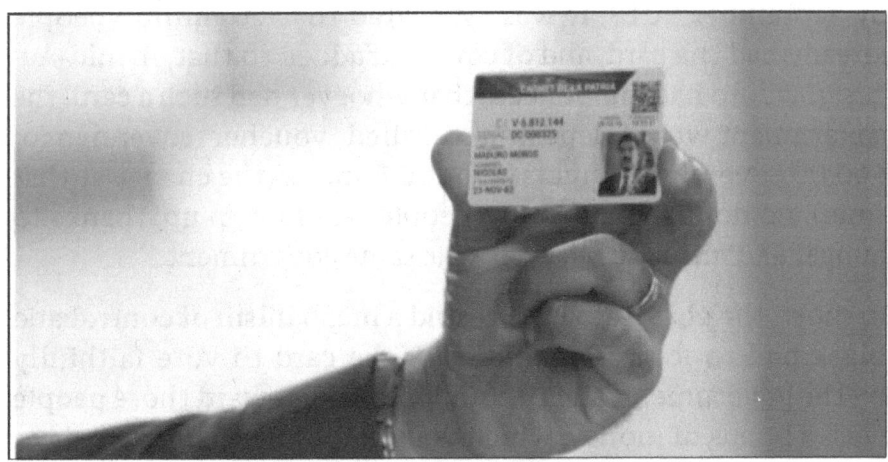

Maduro showing his fatherland card.

Fernando Germán M

In the regional and municipal elections of 2017, as well as in the presidential elections of 2018, the government created a curious voting control mechanism. From the government, the voters were urged to vote with the card. The Chavista government said that whoever had the card to vote, the person would then receive a gift, which consisted, in what the government called, an "economic bonus." According to some opposition leaders, that bonus was an income of about 10 million Bolivars to each person, as a reward for fidelity to the revolutionary process.

So, to know who was or not with his card to vote in favor of the government, in places near the polling stations, were placed some so-called "red spots" of control or supervision, where people, with their card, First I had to go there before going to vote, scan the card, then go to vote at the voting center, where they would give you a voucher, and then, with that voucher, go to the so-called "red dot", and present it, as proof that he voted for the government. Later, the government gave the gift of the bonus, which was not enough to buy a liter of milk. That is, many Venezuelans "sold their vote" for less than a liter of milk.

By September 2018, it was estimated that 10 million people already had the card, and of course, if added to that, in mid-August, Maduro had announced, that whoever had such a card, the government would deposit a so-called "voucher" sovereign "of 600.00 Sovereign Bolivars (about 6 Euros to the change at that time), no doubt, many more people would sign up, thanks to hunger and misery, created by the same government.

In short, the chavismo has created a mechanism of control and blackmail to force the holders of the card to vote faithfully by the government, and in compensation, reward those people with a bonus of money, which does not allow to live two days. And on the other hand, if you do not show your fidelity to the regime, you are condemned to die of hunger.

VENEZUELAN OIL AS A FI-NANCING WEAPON

For many, with Chávez, the so-called "populism" was born, where a so-called political leader offers magical solutions to all problems. But those solutions, more than solutions, are pure fantasy. One example is that Chávez, for everything, focused on solutions within the so-called "Bolivarian revolution", and on looking for a cause of the problems, that is, the culprit. The question is that for the new revolution, the culprit was anyone who did not support the "revolutionary project", and above all, its "commander".

Thus, in Venezuela, starting in 1999, there was an enemy, whom the "supreme commander" called "escualido". Today, with Nicolas Maduro, the name of the enemy has been changed, and now they call it "international right", "Colombian right", "Spanish right", "the United States", "the fascists", or the so-called "economic war" "

This last "excuse" of the so-called "economic war" gives me some laughter, since I wonder, how can there be a war, if for years, there are no solid companies in Venezuela, and the few that remain, the to confiscated the government, in the name of the "revolution". In short, one more excuse, like the one invented by his Cuban allies, when he said that Cubans always go hungry, thanks to the "embargo", or the blockade of the US. What the Cuban government does not count is that on the island, every year, more than two million tourists enter, with their portfolios full of dollars, staying in luxury hotels of five-star Spanish chains, where those tourists do not pass the slightest need, and where the restaurants , they are very full of food. To give an idea of the contrast of the Cuban reality, according to official figures of the Catrist regime, in 2008 2.3 million tourists arrived on the island, which generated to the government an income of 2,700 million dollars. Was that money taken away by the US embargo? Nooot ... that money was taken by the high offices of the Cuban Communist Party to their bank accounts in Switzerland, or other tax havens.

The same situation occurs with Venezuela. Well ... there is a small difference ... Venezuela does not live on tourism. He lives from his oil reserves, which, Chávez, part, dedicated himself to give to his Cuban, Bolivian, Nicaraguan, Ecuadorian friends, etc. That is, to his strategic friends in the area, who, with the so-called "petro-dollars", helped them win elections in those countries. And if not, ask the Kirchner family in Argentina.

Chávez in the company of the Kirchner family.

Argentina? And what does Chávez have to do with Argentina? It happens that between the years 2005 to 2008, Chávez decided to make a juicy business in the name of Venezuela, to buy some

5,600 million dollars of "junk" bonds of the Argentine debt. And how much did Venezuela lose in that business? Well, to this day, nobody knows. The only sure thing is that Venezuela won nothing. Well, what Chávez was looking for on that occasion was for the Argentine government to ally itself with its expressionist policies in the region. That is to say, to have one more country that pamper him as the world leader.

By the way, Chávez signed several agreements to send oil to Argentina, and of which, today, there are many doubts. Well ... the only certain thing is that as always, Venezuela is the one who loses millions of dollars in the business.

THE CHAVISTA PRESENCE IN THE REST OF THE WORLD

Billions of dollars, and millions of barrels of oil, went to the hands of their allies of what is now called the ALBA (Bolivarian Alliance for the Peoples of Our America). A project 100% created by Chavez, and where I insist, billions of dollars were wasted, while within Venezuela itself, the country fell apart.

Chávez, had in mind, his personalist project to be considered a leader in America. And for that, he created regional organizations under his personal direction. And for the task of managing to a large extent the role of these organizations, Chávez handpicked his "political dolphin" Nicolás Maduro.

Billions of dollars, and millions of barrels of oil and food, went to the hands of their allies of the ALBA or Petrocaribe, while within Venezuela itself, the country fell apart.

Chávez, despite being a communist, had seen the failure of the rise of revolutionary armed movements in the region. So, instead of sending arms to Nicaragua, Bolivia, Uruguay, Ecuador, as Cuba did in the 60s, he thought that since he had the largest oil reserves in the world, he could use the "Petrodollars" to finance political parties in the region, and thus, in a "democratic" way, to mount his "Bolivarian empire". The problem is that one thing is to help finance parties to ends, and that these win the elections, and another thing, is that those parties and friendly friends faithful to Chavism, can stay in power in these countries.

For example, in Uruguay, José Mujica won the elections in his country in 2010. Mujica had a reputation for his guerrilla past, since he had been part of the National Liberation Movement - Tupamaros. Years later, in the 2009 elections, he was elected president. And some wonder ... and where did the money for your campaign come from?

The opposition National Party of Uruguay, in August 2009, two months before the elections, had reported that they were going to investigate whether an export of books to Venezuela for more than 32 million dollars was a facade to finance Mujica's campaign, since there were different "suspicious matters" in the transaction. According to the investigation, it was indicated, for example, that the cost of each book "would have been less than 10 dollars and sold at about 498 dollars, so we have a differ-ence close to 30 million dollars in this operation, something which is totally unusual in what has to do with business of any kind." To all this is added, coincidence, that the company that made the business, Apliser S.A., was founded a year earlier, by a cousin of Senator Lucia Topolansky, wife of José Mujica.

José Mujica and Hugo Chávez.

In short, since the arrival of Uruguayan leftist forces in 2005, the commercial exchange between Caracas and Montevideo skyrocketed almost 1,500% to some 741 million dollars in

2009, according to official Venezuelan figures. Almost 100% of Venezuela's exports correspond to energy products, including more than 40,000 barrels of oil per day, while Uruguay sends in exchange dairy products, beef and medicines. So, there is no doubt, ask yourself, how much of those Petrodollars sent by Chávez, was destined to illegally finance the campaign of Mujica?. By the way, to this day, I have not seen the first medication in a Venezuelan pharmacy with the "Made in Uruguay" label.

And behind the signing of all those agreements for the delivery of oil, trade, or the sending of black money to finance electoral campaigns in other countries, without a doubt, Foreign Minister Nicolás Maduro played a key role. In fact, Chávez had designated him precisely for that purpose: To create a network of corruption on a large scale in all the countries of the area, with the sole purpose of assembling, and consolidating friendly governments loyal to the Bolivarian revolution.

Chávez, Evo, Lula, and Correa.

As for Bolivia, Evo Morales became president in January 2006.

His previous life was linked as an active member of a union of coca growers. Thus, what could be understood, that part of their financing of their political life, is closely related to sectors linked to the production of coca in that country. And to this, also, the possible financing from Venezuela is added. Later, after winning the elections, in his first visit to Caracas in 2006, Morales signed seven bilateral agreements, including one for the supply of 200,000 barrels of oil a day, the first of a series of agreements to come. Undoubtedly, in the signing of all these economic, commercial agreements, is behind the signature of Nicolás Maduro.

In El Salvador, as early as 2008, there were allegations that the Farabundo Marti National Liberation Front (FFMLN), a former guerrilla group in El Salvador and the main opposition party, were financed by Chávez. Moreover, thanks to this, the Salvadoran guerrilla came to power in 2009. That a guerrilla group, overnight, get millions of dollars out of nothing, to finance an electoral campaign and win an election, Without a doubt, he has something suspicious.

After coming to power in El Salvador, José Luis Merino, one of the most powerful people in the FFMLN, supervised and led the creation of the Alba Petróleos consortium, financed by PDVSA. Chavez, with his idea of controlling governments with the blackmail of oil, made another version of Petrocaribe for Central America. In other words, with the creation of both consortiums, a form of cover was sought, to finance parties and friends linked to the revolutionary project. How much money did PDVSA get into the FFMLN thanks to Alba Petróleos? Surely Maduro, in his job as chancellor, has some idea of it.

In Nicaragua, after the fall of the Berlin Wall and communism in Europe, the Sandinistas came out of power in 1990. They had come to power in 1979, after a bloody civil war, with support and funding from Cuba. Its leader Daniel Ortega, after the triumph of Chávez, saw the opportunity to regain power. So, in

2006, he returns to power, and today, Nicaragua, lives a kind of internal civil war, where the Sandinistas oppress the people. In April 2018, protests erupted in the country, with a balance of more than 400 deaths until the month of August 2018.

Regarding the dependence on Venezuela, well, it should be noted, that the first act of Ortega's government after his election, was to incorporate Nicaragua to ALBA and Petrocaribe, signing an agreement, where PDVSA committed to cover all fuel needs of Nicaragua at subsidized prices: 50% of the invoice to be paid in 90 days and 50% to a term of 25 years, with two of grace and 2% of interest. Additionally, for the application of the agreement, they opted for a curious modality, where PDVSA decided through a private transaction to deliver 50% of that oil supply to the Caja Rural Nacional (CARUNA), a cooperative controlled by the Sandinista Front.

Chávez and Daniel Ortega.

The agreement represented abundant additional resources for Nicaragua: more than 3,654 million dollars between 2007 and 2016, according to official figures. And all thanks to Petrocaribe. Currently, the opposition in Nicaragua accuses the Sandinistas of receiving millions of dollars from Petrocaribe, which had been used to finance two re-elections of Ortega in 2012 and 2017. How many millions of dollars were allocated from Venezuela for the victories of Ortega ?. Sure, that Maduro, has some idea of it, since part of his work as chancellor from 2006 to 2013, was to negotiate agreements to help its allies in the region.

In the case of Ecuador, Rafael Correa comes to power in 2006, and reelected in the years 2009, and 2013. That is to say, similar to Daniel Ortega, Evo Morales, or Hugo Chávez, all of them, after assuming power, modified their constitutions to be re-elected indefinitely. And of course, all of them have had some help, from a thing called oil. But of all these political leaders, Correa is the only one who has a better professional training. He is an economist, with a doctorate in Belgium, and of course, this has allowed him to have a not-so-fanatical vision of defending Chávez. Moreover, it was the leader of the region who was concerned to some extent for distancing his government from the Chavista model.

The question is that all these pro-revolutionary political leaders in America have copied some things from Chávez. First, the reforms of the constitution and the electoral law in their respective countries, in order to gain more power, and to last longer as leaders. Second, its growing confrontation with the media, and opposition parties, being them, the common enemy to destroy. And third, and most importantly, is the dependence on the oil business, to get money to finance their businesses and electoral campaigns.

In resumed, one could say, that it is a model created, with the end, to give an image of legitimacy in the world, where its leaders use the money of the Venezuelan oil business, to arrive, and perpetuate itself in power.

The issue is that all this scenario, where the Chavez regime contributed to the emergence in several countries of the region of governments allied to Chavismo, is not only Chávez's work. Undoubtedly, the role played by the Venezuelan Chancellor, Nicolás Maduro, between 2006 and 2013, has been of the utmost importance, since he is the one who, to a large extent, was responsible for carrying out the negotiations in the signatures of the agreements commercials, or delivery of oil, or various supplies to the countries of the Chavez axis. And I go further ... Maduro, knew perfectly the illegal financing to pro-Chavez extremist groups in third countries. That was his main role as chancellor, and Chávez appointed him precisely for that.

In Colombia, the Revolutionary Armed Forces (FAR), were on more than one occasion, defended in public by Chavez, and by his Foreign Minister Maduro, and there is no doubt about the financing of Venezuelan Petrodollars to guerrilla groups. In fact, the government of Colombia for years has insisted that the guerrillas hide in Venezuelan territory, protected by the Venezuelan army, and that from Venezuela, they enter Colombia committing attacks, or kidnappings, and return to Venezuela. But there is more ... already in 2018, in the last presidential elections in Colombia, Nicolás Maduro, openly stated his support for the leftist candidate Gustavo Petro, known for his past as a former member of the M-19 guerrilla. In March 2018, the Venezuelan opposition deputy Rafael Ramírez Colina, had pointed out that Chavista funding for presidential candidates is not a secret, and cites several examples:

"Antonini Wilson's briefcase that carried around $ 800,000 for Cristina Kirchner's campaign in Argentina in 2007; the denunciation in 2009 by the president of the Bolivian Senate, Óscar Ortiz, who assured that the Government of Hugo Chávez financed the campaign of Evo Morales; the revelation in Wikileaks documents of financing provided by the Venezuelan Government to the Nicaraguan Government of Daniel Ortega; or the denunciation of the National Party of Honduras (...) about the intervention of Nicolás Maduro in the recent electoral campaign of that country in support of Salvador Nasralla, preferred candidate of Manuel Zelaya, close ally to Chavismo and Nicolás Maduro."

Even in Spain, the Chavistas have created and financed an "anti-imperialist" party called Podemos. In fact, its leaders have traveled to Venezuela very often to participate in activities to support the Venezuelan regime. Its leader, Pablo Iglesias, has come to affirm on more than one occasion that Venezuela is a true model of democracy. Today, thanks to Chavez's Petrodollars, in 2018, they became the third political force in Spain. Much was said about a collection of more than 3 million dollars, from a foundation of Podemos to the Venezuelan government. In fact, there is something that should be highlighted throughout this story. A political party, which emerges from nowhere, can not be the third force in the country with 5 million votes, overnight. Someone has had to finance them, and sure, it has not been any Spanish financial institution. And sure, that Maduro, has very good faith of it.

In short, the Venezuelan oil business, without a doubt, has helped to defeat democratic governments, and then to establish governments at the end of the Bolivarian revolution. And all this, is not achieved, if behind there is no one to organize it. And that someone, in my opinion, was to a large extent, the Venezuelan Chancellor Nicolás Maduro. It is perhaps because of this that Chávez named him as his successor.

THE CHAVISTA INCURSION IN SPANISH POLITICS

In Spain I had to experience the rise of a populist political party, called Podemos, which according to various sources, was financed by the Chavistas. The question is that this "Chavista" party in just two years, became the third political force. And to top it off, its top leader, Pablo Iglesias, says to the four winds, that Venezuela "is one of the healthiest democracies in the world." That is to say, it can be perfectly understood that said party, its ideological model, is based on Chavism. Surely they will tell me that I exaggerate with that affirmation. But to clarify the doubts, I am going to quote you one of the many phrases of a revolutionary court type pronounced by Iglesias. In part from an interview on a television channel in October 2014, he said the following: "A government can not go out one day and abolish the market economy, you can not, I would like to (...) We are very small to load us capitalism alone, for that we would need to Podemos throughout the world." Let's see, now that it sounds to them that it is 100% Chavista ideology?.

The other tragic aspect of the Spanish theme is that in 2018, the Podemos party governs in some municipalities (for example, Madrid and Barcelona), and forms government coalitions in some regions. In fact, there is a fact of great consequences where they played a leading role. In mid-2018, together with the separatist or separatist radical parties, they formed a government coalition to put the "Useless" of Pedro Sánchez of the Socialist Party as president of government in Spain. That is, the Spanish Chavistas, have had the influence to remove a legitimate government elected at the polls (Mariano Rajoy), and put the "puppet" Sanchez, who came "through the back door", without winning an election, and who the podemistas bribe all the days, telling him that if he does not accept his requests, they would stop supporting him, and with that, new elections would be called.

Certainly, there are those who doubt, if in fact, Pablo Iglesias, has served as a shadow president, since he is the one who takes the initiative in announcing economic measures. Thus, in 2018, in Spain there is a "Chavista" radical taking important decisions on behalf of the Spanish government.

By the way, after being elected deputy Mr. Iglesias, one of the first things he did, was to buy a villa of 268 m2 on a plot of 2,000 m2, with its pool, in one of the most expensive areas of Madrid. In short, it is noted, that being a revolutionary Chavista, goes very well with its principles. While on the one hand, gives his great speech that we must defend the so-called "squatters" (people who invade and illegally occupies houses), on the other hand, he, in his big house, does not want to see one. That is to say, according to him, his house is sacred, and it is not touched. His new house is so special, that I believe, that he is one of the few Spanish deputies, who have assigned him policemen of civilians near his house as a special escort. But according to his Chavista ideology, the houses of others, can be invaded or illegally occupied by their comrades or squatters.

But where did Pablo Iglesias come from? Well ... his origins in politics was in the Communist Party of Spain, which, he separated, because according to his radical vision, the party was very soft. Later, he was dabbling in the world of television, grabbing some fame for his radical leftist position. In 2014, with a group of friends, create Podemos, participating in elections to the European Parliament, and getting that party, five seats.

That is to say, in less than a year, he founded a party, and won 5 seats in Europe. And the logical thing to ask in this case, is that to mount a political party from nothing, and spend money on campaign, the money has had to emerge of somewhere. And most likely, it has not been of the militants of his party.

The question is that no one doubts Chavez's relations with the origins of Podemos, since it is more than proven that some of the founders of the party received money from the Venezuelan government.

In the middle of 2017, a Spanish digital media called okdiario.com, presented an interesting report, which indicated that Hugo Chávez, and later Nicolás Maduro, financed with at least 7,765,000 Euros the main leaders and founders of Podemos, in the months and years prior to the creation of the party.

The report states that "According to the documents revealed by OKDIARIO, Maduro's government ordered in February 2014 to pay 272,325 dollars (around 220,000 euros) to the current general secretary of Podemos, Pablo Iglesias, in a Euro Pacific Bank account in fiscal paradise of the San Vicente and Grenadines Islands. "For this, Okdiario presents a copy of the payment order of the Venezuelan government.

And before this news, what has Mr. Iglesias done? Well, to denounce the journalist who published the information, and the result of that complaint, was that he lost it, since the court in charge of it, came to the conclusion that the news was "truthful, contrasted and of general interest".

On the other hand, in the report of Okdiario, it is noted that one of the founders of Podemos, Juan Carlos Monedero, collected 425 thousand euros from Banco Alba, controlled by the Chavista regime. According to the newspaper, Monedero claims that he collected the money "for writing a report on the implementation of a single currency in the countries of the Chavista orbit. A report that has never seen the light and that, according to all indications, has never existed. Previously, Monedero had worked for at least three years at the Miraflores Palace as a personal adviser to Hugo Chávez. "

The web newspaper Okdiario, on the other hand indicates that "it has published the evidence that Nicolás Maduro personally signed the order to pay another 142,000 dollars (around 120,000 euros) to three prominent members of the direction of Podemos: the deputies Carolina Bescansa, Ariel Jerez and Jorge Lago". In theory, the three deputies of Podemos charged this amount for preparing the "communicational political design of the audiovisual material" for the stand of the state-owned company Petróleos de Venezuela SA (PDVSA) at the XXI World Petroleum Congress held in June of 2014 in Moscow".

And finally, in the investigative report, it states that "In a sworn statement, former Venezuelan Finance Minister Rafael Isea has confirmed before the Spanish Police that Hugo Chávez ordered in 2008 to pay 6.7 million dollars (about 6 million euros) to the CEPS Foundation (Center for Political and Social Studies), whose patrons were part of the main founders of Podemos in Spain: "Pablo Iglesias, Íñigo Errejón, Carolina Bescansa, Rita Maestre, Alberto Montero and Luis Alegre, among others." For this, the web newspaper provides as proof a copy of the document signed by Chávez. Okdiario affirms that Chávez "orders to pay this amount to the CEPS Foundation to propitiate [in Spain] a political change even closer to the Bolivarian government". And he specifically mentions the names of Pablo Iglesias, Juan Carlos Monedero and Jorge Verstrynge as "natural allies of the Bolivarian revolution."

According to Okdiario, "In exchange for this money, the members of CEPS prepared reports to advise the Hugo Chávez regime on how to repress the opposition, how to improve their communication and even suggested what issues to address in their Aló Presidente program. "

In short, with the report of Okdiario, it is shown that the leaders of Podemos, before the creation of the party in 2014, had already collected 7.7 million euros from the Chavez regime.

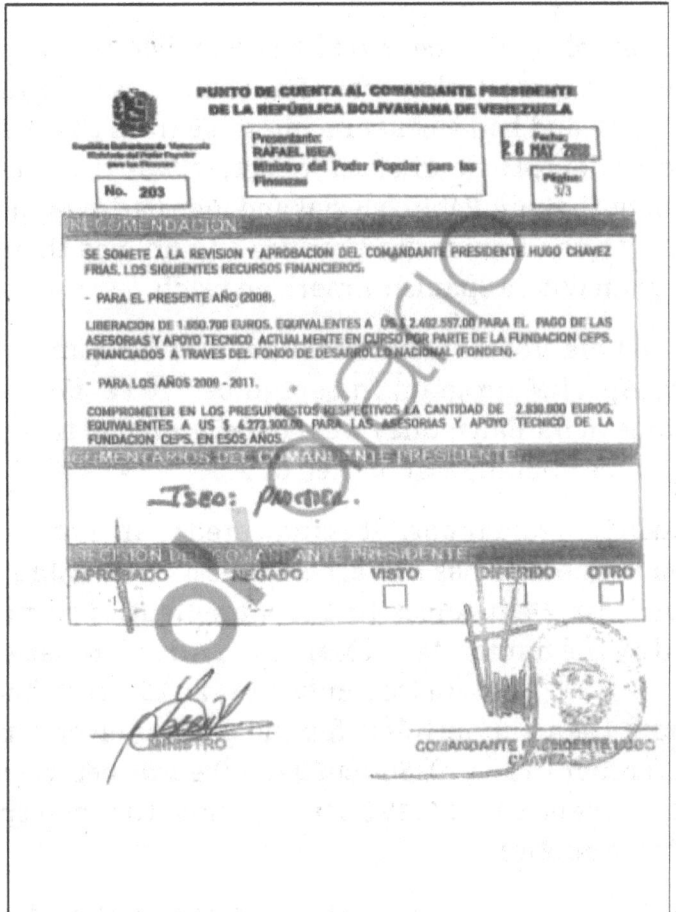

Order of payment to the CEPS Foundation signed by Chávez.

But I insist, a political party, of ultra left, that does not believe in the banks and the private sector, out of nothing, and overnight, can not become the third political force of a country, and spend millions of euros in electoral campaigns, if there is no one behind with hidden interests. The money comes from somewhere. Some people point out that they are also financed by Iran. And you will wonder what Iran has to do with Podemos ?.

Mr. Iglesias has his own television programs, and one of them, called "Fort Apache", was financed by that country, since it was broadcast on the Iranian public television station Hispan TV.

At the beginning of June 2016, the Spanish newspaper ABC published a report, stating that "The chain was inaugurated in January 2012 and had a welcome message from the then Venezuelan president, Hugo Chávez. In fact, it was the Venezuelan government that put Pablo Iglesias and Juan Carlos Monedero in contact with the Iranians to produce and finance their television program with a Spanish-American reach.

Iglesias and his closest team of collaborators began producing the "Fort Apache" program in September 2012, although the first income of Iranian money were in December of that year, according to the documents collated by ABC. "

Additionally, in said report, it is indicated that "The documentation to which ABC has had access reveals that Pablo Iglesias issued at least 24 invoices to the aforementioned producer, managed by the Iranian Azimi Mahmoud Alizadeh, between December 28, 2012. and on November 11, 2015, when there was little more than a month left for the general elections of 20-D (20 dicember in Spain). Suman 97,610 euros net, to which is added 21 percent VAT (20,498.10 euros) and the corresponding withholding applies.

The question is that it is not clear, what was the fate of that money. And what is suspected is that part was destined to the foundation or financing of Podemos. And if that has been the case, then we would be facing the crime of illegal financing of a Spanish political party, with funds from foreign governments (Venezuela and Iran).

One day, it will be discovered that the Russians, experts in meddling in electoral campaigns like those of the US or France, also helped Podemos. And I think they have certainly done something, since the Russians are very close friends of the Venezuelan Chavez regime.

At the end of 2017, in a commission of investigation of political parties made by the Spanish Senate, the former partner of Pablo Iglesias, and director of Channel 33, Enrique Riobóo, had accused Iglesias of founding Podemos with money from Venezuela and Iran. In this commission of investigation, Riobóo indicated that Iglesias and Monedero had the "full pockets" of money from these countries. For the businessman, Podemos would not have achieved five europarlamantarios in 2014 without funds received from abroad, of which he was "witness" for the relationship he had with them from his position in the channel that issued "La Tuerka" (Another program of Pablo Iglesias TV).

Also, in said commission of inquiry, Mr. Monedero was quoted, who acknowledged having collected a total of 425,150 euros from the governments of Bolivia, Nicaragua, Venezuela and Ecuador, for advisory work to implement a common currency.

By the way, in 2016, the Parliament with an opposition majority in Venezuela, also created its commission of investigation on the financing of Podemos, and invited Mr. Iglesias to go to Caracas to clarify doubts. The issue is that it seems that Mr. Iglesias has no illusions about going to a commission of inquiry in Venezuela.

But the big question in all this issue, is how much money was moved by tax havens for the financing and creation of a party with Chavista ideology in Spain?.

In mid-January 2016, according to an investigation by the Spanish police, the so-called "communication network of Podemos", had received 2.4 million Euros from Iran in 4 years. And before the accusations that the ones of Podemos have said: that all that money has been limited to the production of the television program "Fort Apache", a television program, that at most, would have an audience of 30 people.

In mid-February 2016, the Spanish police presented a report to the Spanish Court of Audit, where it is deduced that there is sufficient evidence to act on behalf of the tribunal against Podemos. After the first investigations of said court, in August of 2017, the latter stated that he wished to know who finances Podemos, since said political organization, always alleged, that its financing is based on the voluntary aid of its followers. After this pressure from the court, the podemistas presented their list of donors, where there are about 500, who present serious doubts. And you will say what doubts ?. Very easy. That list includes many people who earn less than 12 thousand euros a year, and who have donated between 1 thousand and 5 thousand euros. Someone believes that people with low income donate these large amounts of money ?. Finally, in Spain that practice is known as "pitufeo". That is, use many people who make small bank transfers to launder money, in this case, hypothetically, money from Venezuela or Iran.

I insist ... to create a political party at European level, and be the third political force in Spain, they have had to spend a lot of money, and that money, it does not come from the political party militants Podemos. Still, in 2018, it is not very clear, how the creation and growth of that Chavista party was financed. But I am sure, that one day not very far, the truth will come out, and more than one, it will take its great surprise.

So that you have an idea, that Chavista influence reaches far into Podemos, I'm going to tell you a curious thing. After getting 67 deputies in the Spanish Parliament in 2016, the podemistas "promised" their deputy position with this phrase: "I promise to abide by this Constitution and work to change it " This phrase, repeated, and completed, by all elected deputies of Podemos, is inspired by that used by Hugo Chávez seventeen years before, when the "commander" swore as president saying: "I swear before God, before the country and before my people , about this moribund Constitution, which I will enforce and promote the necessary democratic transformations so that the new Republic has a Magna Carta appropriate to the times ". Both formulas have one aspects in common: the promise to reform the Constitution.

And to finish this topic, I am going to tell you another fact, which shows, how ultra chavista is Mr. Iglesias. In 2013, after the death of the "comandante", Iglesias was in charge of presenting an act of homage to Chávez in Madrid. In this event, the leader of Podemos said that "Hugo Chávez was the democracy of the underdogs, Hugo Chávez was democracy, it was a scandal for the powerful, that is why they feared him and continue to fear him."

The Spanish Communist leader Pablo Iglesias, in the center, accompanied by two Chavistas leaders in Madrid, Spain, in an act of homage to Hugo Chavez in 2016.

In short: the Chavistas in Spain had achieved the goal of a political change by setting up a new government more akin to the Bolivarian regime, and all this thanks to the petrodollars financing from Caracas, to create overnight, the third political force in Spain in 2018. That political force called Podemos, together with the socialists and radical groups, between May and June of 2018, orchestrated what many would call "a military coup" against a legitimate government that had clearly won an election.

At the beginning of 2019, the Spanish Chavistas, largely support the government of socialist Pedro Sanchez. Such was the dominion of Pablo Iglesias over Sánchez, that when they asked the socialist "leader" about the crisis in Venezuela, he left with the same speech as his party colleague, Rodríguez Zapatero. That is to say, he said that the solution in Venezuela was dialogue.

But all this changed from the end of January 2019, after the emergence of Guaidó as president in Venezuela, making this fact, forced Sanchez to change an opinion turn to his regret, and all thanks to the pressure of the opposition politics in Spain, and also to international pressure, and more, when the European Parliament itself gave its support to Guaidó.

And in front of the new position of Spain on Venezuela, which the gentlemen of Podemos have said, and the radical Spanish left ... Well, that Venezuela is a democracy, and that the Maduro regime supports without fissures.

Finally ... with what happened in Spain in mid-2018 (Motion of censure against Mariano Rajoy), it is demonstrated that with the money of the petro-dollars of Venezuela in the hands of the radical left, governments can be overthrown and mounted. In fact, the Chavistas had already applied it to a large extent in Bolivia, Ecuador, Nicaragua, or El Salvador. And we must not forget the new Mexican case, where a new ally of Maduro, Mr. Andrés Manuel López Obrador, came to power. And all thanks to ...

My hope is that, as events are going, the Caracas regime is no longer able to continue funding the creation of "chavista" parties around the world. There are not so many petrodollars anymore. Surely, in the next elections in Spain, the lords of Podemos, will have a strong collapse of votes. And when Mr. Iglesias call desperate his allies in Caracas to ask for help of money, surely someone will tell on behalf of Maduro the following: Pablito, there is no money!

Pedro Sánchez and Pablo Iglesias, until the end of January 2019,
allies in the defense of the Bolivarian Revolution in Spain.

THE OIL CHAOS IN VENEZUELA

While Chávez devoted himself to buying countries with the shipment of Venezuelan oil, to the Venezuelan oil installations, in 20 years of Chavismo, they were not given adequate maintenance since the arrival of the "revolution", with which the country has drastically reduced its production, not for lack of oil, if not, for the closure of oil facilities due to poor maintenance. On the other hand, it is noteworthy that all the facilities are in conditions of maximum insecurity, and with the fear that at any moment, a human tragedy may occur.

To give an example, on August 12, 2012, there was a tragic explosion at the Amuay refinery in northern Venezuela. This explosion caused 55 deaths, and of course, the closure of said refinery (one of the five largest in the world in 1997). According to the "official" excuse of the government, about the cause of said explosion, "it was lightning." Interestingly, that day in the area did not rain, nor were there storm predictions. On the other hand, they gave another official version, that the cause was a gas leak, with which, it was recognized that the facilities operated without the minimum guarantees of proper maintenance. And to top it off, on the other hand, and to somehow justify, that the government is not responsible for the tragedy, the vice president of PDVSA and vice minister of Petroleum and Mines for that year, Eulogio del Pino, said in an interview with the State television network VTV, which did not rule out the thesis of sabotage as the cause of the explosion. In short, if something goes wrong in Venezuela, the fault is never the government's.

Let's see if they understand me ... a country, which in 1970, produced 3.5 million barrels a day, we find that in August 2018, it hardly produces 1.5 million. Whose fault is it?. Of the "revolutionary" government that in more than 20 years dedicated itself to giving oil to its friendly countries of ALBA, and has ruined the main oil industry in the world called Petróleos de Venezuela (PDVSA)?; or is it the fault of the "escualidos", or of the US?

Explosion at the Amuay refinery in 2012.

Today PDVSA in a ruined company, with billions of dollars in debt. And do you know where that debt is concentrated today? ... in China and Russia, allied countries of the Bolivarian revolution, just because of the "business". Of course, it's a big business, since those governments, they charge that debt, with the reserves of Venezuelan oil, which later, China and Russia, offer it to third countries, as if it were Chinese and Russian oil. And all thanks to the signatures of various agreements, such as the one made with Russia in September 2008, with which that country managed to strengthen its business, or rather, its strategic position, in the American continent.

As for environmental tragedies, for some years, oil spills have been reported in various rivers of Venezuela, and in the face of complaints, the government, what it has done, is to minimize, or silence the complainants.

An example of this was what happened at the beginning of November 2016, when after the rupture of a Petroanzoategui pipeline, more than 25 thousand barrels of oil were spilled in a river in the Anzoategui region. According to the first investigations, the cause was the lack of maintenance and investment.

According to the human rights body Provea, official figures indicate that in Venezuela, the number of oil spills has increased, from 2,369 cases in 2010 to 10,660 in 2013. And the most striking of all is that both PDVSA, like the Chavez government itself, have not bothered to take measures to prevent further ecological disasters, and worse, when they find out about one, they do not take the slightest steps to clean up the affected areas.

THE FALL OF THE TOURISM IN-
DUSTRY IN VENEZUELA

During my stay in Spain, one of the things that many Spaniards told me is that Venezuela has a privileged position because of its geographical location. A land with virgin beaches, snowy mountains, deserts, rivers, jungle, with cities with colonial architecture ... elements that make the country attractive for international tourism. That is to say, there are good products to offer, but unfortunately, the government, what it has done, is to drive away, or rather, to scare away tourists. A route of arrival of foreign tourists to the country is by air, and it seems that the government is more interested in closing airlines, than to facilitate the arrival of more tourists with money to the country. A direct consequence of this closure is the bankruptcy and ruin of many companies in the country, which live directly or indirectly from tourism. An example of this are hotels, tourist groups, travel agencies, etc., companies that gave employment to thousands of Venezuelans.

So much so that the Chavista regime wants to look like Cuba, that they forget, that one of the main pillars that help in some way to maintain the communist regime on the island, is the income obtained with tourists' dollars.

In the case of the airlines that fly to Venezuela, it happens that the Chavista government, for years, has multi-million dollar debts with these companies. And how is that? ... well ... imagine you live in Venezuela, and want to buy a ticket to travel outside the country. The government forces to sell to the airlines the local currency plane tickets, the Bolívar. The problem is that foreign airlines, to travel to Venezuela, spend of their pockets of dollars or euros, while in Venezuela, in their offices, have billions of bolivars of the sales of tickets, bolivars that are worth

nothing in Venezuela

The question is that this amount in Bolivars, the Venezuelan government, has to change it to the companies, in dollars at the price of an official change fixed by the government itself, which is very, very inferior to the reality of the market, with which, the airlines, lose millions of dollars. And the most comical of the case, is that the government recognizes a debt, and does not know, if someday it will pay. The issue is that with so many claims from the companies with the threat that if they do not pay the debt, they will not fly, the response of the Venezuelan government is that if they stop flying, it will be forever, and that if, forget about Debt.

Preparations for the takeoff of the last flight of Delta Air Lines, after announcing its closure of operations in Venezuela in September 2017.

In the case of Air Italia, in 2015 it stopped flying, since the government owed them more than 177 million dollars. So together with the Italians,, have joined Aeromexico, Air Canada,

Lufthansa, KLM, Avianca, United Airlines, Delta, Aerolineas Argentinas, etc, and the few that still fly to Venezuela, have drastically reduced their flights.

In March 2014, Maduro recognized a debt of more than 3,800 million dollars. Today, for some followers of the revolution, Maduro has managed to lower that debt, not because of the fact that they have paid something, but because of the fact that the companies that have left have lost their right to claim that debt.

And so, as in the case of airlines, all the other companies that depend on foreign currency to operate in Venezuela work. And as the government controls every dollar that moves in the country, it will be understood, because there is a total chaos of supplies of medicines, food, spare parts for vehicles, etc.

Another detail ... Venezuela is the country, where airport taxes are the most expensive in the world. To give an example. In 2018, a passenger from Madrid to Venezuela, pays about 20.00 Euros of fees when leaving from Spain. But if you leave from Caracas to Madrid, the revolutionary government charges fees of 500.00 Euros! Thus, it will be understood that Venezuela has the most expensive plane tickets in the world, and not precisely, it is the fault of the airlines, if not of the same government, which seeks to obtain more dollars to finance its revolution.

So with the policy of scare the airlines, it will be understood that the number of tourists has fallen a bit in recent years. If we add to this aspects, for example, that Caracas is the most violent city in the world, it is that even if a foreign tourist wants to enjoy a beach in Venezuela, it is to be thought 20 times. It is perhaps that many foreign tourists choose to travel, for example, to Cuba.

MY TRIP TO CUBA

In 1999, I met some Cuban boys who studied at the university, and of course, we always talked about various topics, and when the issue of politics came up, I told them, if we wanted to keep friendship, it is better to talk about sports, or another topic. After mid-year, the holiday season arrived, and they were returning to Cuba, and I had planned to go to Venezuela. One of them told me that if I traveled with Cubana de Aviación, stopping in Havana, the ticket would be cheaper, and if I went, they could pick me up at the airport, and show me the benefits of the revolution.. I researched with a travel agency, and it turned out that in truth, It was cheaper to travel to Venezuela, stopping in Havana.. The boys left, and I bought the air ticket.

But before getting on the plane, I had to process a tourist visa, to be able to walk around the island. So one day, I went to the Cuban consulate in Madrid, and upon entering, I found a waiting room, where I saw something that made me curious. There were about five couples, all of them, of Spanish men over 40 or 50 years old, accompanied by Cuban girls who did not exceed 25 years. I asked someone there, and they told me that those couples were there, to process their marriages. Anyway, I thought it was weird, but in short, each one with his life.

When I arrive at the window for the processing of the visa, they ask me how many times I will enter and leave Cuba. I told them I was going from Madrid to Havana, that I would make a stopover before going to Caracas, and that on that scale, some friends would pick me up at the airport, to take me for a walk, and that on the way back from Caracas, it would possibly happen, the same. So the Consulate official tells me, that for this, he would need two visas. And I ask him why, and he tells me, every time he comes and goes, I have to have a visa. That is to say, it is not like the rest of the countries, where for example, visas are for a period of time, and not for each entry or ladder of the country. For example, within the European Union (EU), tourist visas last 90 days, and in those 90 days, you can enter and leave the EU as many times as you want. What's more, imagine you arrive in Madrid, spend 60 days, travel to Morocco for 30 days, and return to Barcelona. Well, even though you spent 30 days in Morocco, you still have 30 days to be legally in the EU. That is, you can be in Barcelona, Berlin, or Paris, without problems. Well, in Cuba, history is something else. So, with resignedly, I told the official, for now, to give me a visa, and that if during my stay in Havana everything went well, then in Caracas, I would process the other visa for the return.

I asked how much was the cost, and they told me about 30 US dollars. At that time, I had in my wallet Pesetas, which circulated as official currency in Spain at that time, and told the official, if he could pay the equivalent in Pesetas. Answer: he tells me, that only American dollars are accepted, and that in any case, go to a house of exchange, and return with the dollars. In short, this was my first impression of Cuba, a country that shouts to the four winds that it is anti-imperialist, and on the other hand, it asks for dollars from its citizens, or foreigners, for some paperwork.

Once the visa process has been completed, and after informing my friends of the day and time of arrival in Havana, the day of the flight arrives. After passing the controls of the Madrid airport, and getting on the plane, I was very surprised, because when I sat down and saw the inside of the plane, I found that it was a very modern airplane, practically luxury. I had already traveled with other companies, and of course, that brand new luxury airplane had left me stunned. I thought that possibly, I had ridden on the wrong plane. So, I saw a stewardess, and I asked her if that plane is from Cubana de Aviación, and she answered me, no. In fact, the plane is rented by Cubana de

Aviación. Finally, with that answer, all my doubts were clarified.

I arrive in Havana, and after disembarking, I go to the queue to have my passport stamped, and the cuban official asks me where I am going to stay. I informed him that some friends were out waiting for me, and that I would stay less than a day on the island, since in the end I had to take another flight to Caracas. The official, he tells me, that by regulation, during the first day of stay, I have to stay in a hotel. I told him, that in my case, I did not need it, since on the same day I was leaving. But the more he said no, he insisted that if he wanted to I leave the airport, he had to pay for a hotel day, even if he did not need it. So, they retained my passport, and after a while, I see that there is another group of tourists, who like me, had they were retained with the same story of the hotel. Then another official tells us that could provide us with a list of hotels. I asked him which was the most economical, and he tells me that the cheapest one is a room shared with three people, and that it costs around 50 American dollars per person. I told him that the price was very expensive. I told him that a shared room, in the center of Madrid, with hot water, costs about 30 dollars. I he thought it was a robbery. Anyway, I told him I could pay now, and forget about it. But the official tells me that paying now is not possible, since I would have to go to the hotel, fill out the paper of the reservation, pay there at the hotel. And I said "Que!" Well ... inhale a breath of air, endure, and I said to myself inside me .... calm ... calm ... So my next question was if the hotel was far away, and the cuban official tells me that I would have to Go out and take a taxi, and that would cost about 50 American dollars. And I told her, that's what she tells me now, but the truth is that if I go out, and the taxi driver comes up with the idea that they are 100 dollars! So, I told him, because I do not have so much money to spend, the truth is that I'd rather stay at the airport. So, the official took my passport, and transferred me to the transfer area, to take the other flight to Caracas. There, I told him that I would have to phone my friends, to let them know I could not leave the airport. The answer was that I bought a phone card, which does it cost 10 US dollars, for me to make a local call that costs about 30 cents. I mean, to make a local call, I had to spend 10 dollars! So, I did not call my friends. Then, I said, that since I was going to be in an area without restaurants, the logical thing is that I would have to eat somewhere. The answer was that the restaurant was on the second floor, and that being on that floor, if I go, technically, I left the airport, and to re-enter to take the flight to Caracas, I would have to pay a rate of 20 Dollars. In short, without having left the airport, the Cuban government wanted to take out all the money.In the end, I had to settle for the cafeteria, where I bought a sandwich, which cost me about 15 dollars, and that in Spain, it cost much less than half the price. I pay with a 20 dollar bill, and then, they give me some Cuban coins instead. I told the one in the cafeteria, that if he paid with dollars, he would give me American coins instead. And the good man tells me, that those currencies, in Cuba, their value is equal to the dollar, and that when I leave, I would have to leave the airport, to make a long line, to exchange them for American dollars. So, I was forced to keep the coins, as an indelible memory of my visit to Cuba.

And even, the good thing of the story has not arrived. It's time to take the flight to Caracas, and we have to get on the plane by some stairs. As I go up, I see the fuselage of the plane, and I notice that it has
paint brush brands marks. As if someone had painted the plane, as if it were the wall of a private house. That left me impressed. You could clearly see the ruts of the past of the brush. What's more, it gives me the idea that they used oil paint, and never, special paint for airplane fuselage. And when I get inside, and I have to sit down, I find a super-gloomy panorama. It was before me, an airplane practically in ruins. The place where I had to sit, the seat next to me, was, and I say it with all certainty, totally destroyed. I never imagined that I would be inside an

old Russian Yak-42D plane. Upon hearing the ignition of the engines, a thick layer of white smoke began to appear inside the cabin, which came out from under the floor. I ask the stewardess what it was, and she told me not to worry, that it was just the airplane's cooling system. So I said to myself ... what a good system ... it has left me cold!.

So, I started the flight to Caracas, peeking looking out the window of the plane, to see if he saw something strange, like flames in the engine of the plane.

And the return trip from Caracas to Cuba, well, I had the same plane, and it was my turn to have to be kidnapped at the Havana airport, waiting for the flight back to Madrid.

After my arrival in Madrid, I told some people about my tragic experience, and almost nobody believed me. The truth is that I did not understand, as the aeronautical authorities of Cuba and Venezuela, allowed those Russian planes completely ramshackle, could fly. The question is that four months after my trip, on December 25, 1999, one of these old Russian planes from Cuba, crashed in Venezuela, with an unfortunate balance of 22 people killed. And in spite of the tragedy, Cubana de Aviación continued to use those ramshackle Russian planes, and accidents continued with tragic deaths. Between March of 2002, and May of 2018, there were 4 Cubana air accidents, with a balance of 203 deaths. And all these accidents point to the use of a dilapidated fleet of aircraft, which do not exceed the minimum quality and maintenance controls. Eye ... that the airplanes that are used for flights to Europe, is something else, since the European authorities, would not allow dilapidated old airplanes over their airspace. That is why Cubana rents planes for those routes.

THE HARDSHIPS OF VENEZUELANS
WHO WANT TO ESCAPE FROM
THE COUNTRY

If we talk about how people have tried to leave Venezuela by air, well, what happened to me with Cubana in Havana, is small.

Between 2017 and 2018, the process to leave the country could be summarized as follows:

The first and foremost is to get a venezolan passport. The interested person has to get into a government website, and from there, make the corresponding request, and pay in advance for the passport. Problem … since 2017, it is practically impossible to enter this web page, since it is hanging, or not going. In my case, to be able to renew the passport, and without exaggerating, I spent almost a whole month, trying to get in every day, and at different times, until at one point, I was able to do the procedure. This was at the beginning of 2018.

The issue is that since 2017, the Chavista government has stated that there are no passports, and that in view of this, they could be extended by processing the website of the Administrative Service of Identification, Migration and Aliens (SAIME). The extension is to pay a sticker, which is printed in Caracas, and sent, as in my case, to a consular office in Spain. That single sticker, cost me about 80.00 Euros, plus another 80.00 Euros that I was asked at the consulate for consular "fees". In short, I paid 160.00 Euros, for a piece of paper that lasts 2 years, and they have stuck it to the expired passport. By the way, in August 2018, the price of the decal was at 280.00 Euros. You how much it costs in Spain to get a new Spanish passport, and that it's for a period of 10 years?: about 30.00 Euros. Yes, 30.00 Euros, while the Venezuelan government, takes out 280.00 Euros, for sticking a piece of paper that lasts two years to the expired passport.

The issue is that the venezolan passport, I needed it, since I was traveling to Brazil. When I arrive at the airport in Sao Paulo in April 2018, and pass through the control of the police entrance, the officer looks at my passport, and all surprised, tells me how I can travel with something expired. I explained the whole story to get the sticker, and the official tells me that according to international standards, that passport is not legal, and as they understand that in Venezuela, there is a "tragic" situation, they let the Venezuelans can enter Brazil without problems.

To another curious fact: Venezuela, was part of MERCOSUR, a kind of version of European Community, where the member citizens, can circulate freely between countries. As a result of the constant violations by the Venezuelan government, MER-COSUR, in August of 2017, suspended the country indefinitely, with which it is deduced that Venezuelans could no longer circulate freely in those countries. So with the background of MER-COSUR, and with the passport "expired" because the Venezuelan government does not print passports, I saw myself in limbo, at the time of entering Brazil, thinking, that I would get stuck to enter. In fact, the Brazilian authorities were fully entitled to not let me in.

Now, imagine another Venezuelan, who wants to get a new passport. As it does? Well, very simple. If you live in Venezuela, your only option is to go to gentile "managers", who for about between 1000 and 2000 dollars US dollars, manage to process a passport with some "contact" within the government. In fact, in my case, when I was desperate because in the website of the government I could not do the procedure of the sticker, someone told me that they could take my passport for 2000 Euros. And I asked why it was so expensive, and the answer was very simple: "is that you live in Europe".

The last passports that were printed by Venezuela are light blue and bear the text MERCOSUR. As Venezuela was expelled, logic-ally, it would be understood that those passports are not valid. But since it's Venezuela, well, you have to turn a blind eye.

After passing of the Venezuelan the passport test, the other step is to get a plane ticket, which is not easy. As I indicated in one of my previous comments, in Venezuela, a large number of foreign airlines have left, and the few that remain have re-duced their flight frequencies. So, if someone wants to travel, for example, within a month, then, it will be an impossible task, since normally, the reservations of the airlines are usually full up to 6 months. That is, it is very difficult, since some airs companies block sales within Venezuelan territory, and only accept sales of tickets, to those who make the purchase outside of Venezuela. And the reason for it. Very easy. The airs com-panies, by law in Venezuela, are obliged to accept the payment of the tickets in Bolivars, in exchange for official government. Then, the companies grab those Bolivars, and take them to the government, so that they can also change for dollars. Problem: The government has not made the change for years, and the airs companies have in their offices, tons of Venezuelan banknotes, which are worthless. Thus, these airs companies are forced to block sales of tickets within Venezuela, and only admit foreign currency purchases outside of Venezuela. And to all this, we must add the airport charges charged by Venezuela, of around 500.00 Euros, which are included in the price of the plane ticket. The incredible thing about this story is that the same passenger, if traveling from Madrid to Caracas, in Spain pays about 20.00 Euros of fees. So, we have, that Venezuela has the most expensive air tickets in the world, thanks to the airport taxes charged by the Chavista revolution.

Then, if the passenger only has the Venezuelan nationality, it is necessary to comply with a series of precautions, if you want to travel, for example to Spain. To enter that country, they ask you to have a one-way ticket and return, no more than a 90-day stay; to have 70.77 euros per person and day of the trip with a minimum of 636.93 euros or its legal equivalent in foreign currency of free convertibility; Reservation of hotel and circuit for the entire stay or letter of invitation; and Travel Insurance. This is only to be able to enter Spain. Another thing, are the procedures to leave Venezuela. For example, they ask for an authorization of official currencies issued by the government. With this, the government wants to know, from where the dollars were taken by the person who is willing to travel. If the government determines that it is of doubtful origin, the money will be confiscated. And as a curiosity, additionally, they ask for bank statements stamped by the bank. This is also, with the idea of controlling by the government, how much money you have the traveler.

And after overcoming the impossible of the passport, getting a plane ticket, and presenting all the bureaucratic procedures, the last step comes to be able to leave the country. Being able to get on the plane. It seems that the last step is simple, but in the case of Venezuela, it is not.

You have to be prepared, for possible extortions by airport officials. More than one, it has happened to him, that he has not taken the famous processed the declaration of the amount of foreign currency that carries over when leaving the country, and of course, as many have obtained currencies on the black market, these are not declared on the return, since They if a person they have bought money on the black market, it is a crime that implies prison sentences. So, when an airport official asks the traveler, how much money habe, there comes the picaresque of the airport official of the "feared" National Guard, by telling the traveler, that if detepta that if he gets more dollars than declared, he runs the risk that they confiscate everything, but that if they cooperate willingly with something, they can turn a blind eye.

And additionally, they imply to you, that if the flight leaves in three hours, the paperwork can take five hours. So that "good-will collaboration" can go between 100 or 1000 dollars. And if the lucky traveler habe pieces of gold, such as chains or rings, stored in your luggage, the airport official he comes up with the story of that the traveler is trafficking in "State property" or "strategic material". So the traveler has two options: give some dollars, or some piece of gold.

After overcoming this control of customs, comes the next step: the power to get a seat available on the plane. And the why of it. Very easy. With few flights, there is always what they call overbooking, that is, the airline usually sells more tickets than seats available inside the plane. And when this happens, the "pintorezca" of the officials of the National Integrated Service of Customs and Tax Administration (SENIAT) of Venezuela goes into action. They approach a traveler, and they tell him that if he does not want to be at the airport for three or four days, hoping to get a free seat on the plane, they can help him solve the problem, that is, in exchange for an "economic collaboration". About $ 100. " They tell the person, that as the first to embark, are the elderly people in a wheelchair. And the lucky traveler asks where he is going to get a wheelchair, and the SENIAT official tells him that he rents it for those 100 dollars, and so, can pass and board directly on the plane, without having to do the dreaded queue .

And after the Venezuelan traveler, having overcome all these obstacles, and arriving in Madrid, we still have to overcome one step. The control of passport entry in Spain, and have the luck, not to be a police control, asking for all the documents, to enter Spain. It is known that many people do not know how, maybe with the help of a good official at the Maiquetía airport in Caracas, they get on the plane, without having the dollars, or euros needed, to justify their stay as a tourist in Spain. So, many travel with crossed fingers. Or, it may be the case, that when the person entered the airport of Maiquetía de Caracas, he had the necessary dollars, but as he was extorted by the Venezuelan authorities, he lost more than half of the money in paying the extortions. Thus, there have been cases of Venezuelans who have arrived in Madrid, and have been returned to Venezuela on the next flight, for lack of the dollars.

And what about those Venezuelans who do not have the opportunity to fly? One of the options is to cross the border of Colombia and Brazil on foot, or in private vehicles; or as in some other cases, to reach the Caribbean islands in private ships or boats of canoes managed by illegal trafficking networks of human beings. In fact, there are people who have died, trying to reach in small rafts to Curaçao. Never in my life, I had thought, that Venezuelans would leave the country practically, swimming. A case that came to light was in early 2018, when the government of Curaçao reported that it had located 10 corpses of Venezuelan "balseros" on its coasts.

According to the International Organization for Migration (IOM), the flow of Venezuelans to Latin America increased by 900% between 2015 and 2017, years in which the number of Venezuelan migrants increased from 89,000 to 900,000. To this, the studies of the UN Agency for Refugees, which presented at the beginning of November 2018, together with the IOM, a new report, which estimates that by that time, had already escaped the country more than three millions of Venezuelans And before the evidence, what Mr. Maduro said? Well, everything is a lie. That there are no Venezuelan refugees. Or that those who have left, the vast majority has returned to Venezuela.

The question is that by last August 2018, the governments of Brazil, Ecuador, and Peru, have hit the shout in the sky, before the arrival of so much Venezuelan to their borders, without documents, and in an "irregular" situation. On the other hand, in those countries, its population has experienced a rejection of the arrival of Venezuelans. One of the causes is that many of those who arrive are in a lamentable situation, without work, without a roof to live in, and as is logical, this has created a humanitarian problem, where various organizations such as the Red Cross, have been overwhelmed by the avalanche of people. Of all the countries affected by the migratory wave, Colombia, perhaps, is the one that has shown the greatest solidarity. The issue is that everything has a limit, and a country, can not accommodate millions of people, and this, has a cost.

And if we talk about Venezuelans escaping to Europe, a similar situation occurs, as the vast majority who travel, for example, to Spain, come asking for political asylum, and of course, the Spanish government, to grant it, does not give it that easy. First, the person who asks for it must prove that he or she is a persecuted person in their country of origin. To give an idea with figures, in 2017, a total of 10,350 Venezuelans sought refuge in Spain, compared to 3,960 in 2016, or 596 in 2015. In 2017, only about 15 Venezuelans achieved refugee status.

So, although you may not believe it, there are currently more than three million Venezuelans outside of their country, who technically are refugees, but for the eyes of some governments, or humanitarian institutions, they are not.

And for Maduro, everything is going well, since no one talks about refugees, or exiles, and that is a problem that does not interest him.

By the way, not all Venezuelans who escape from the country are opponents of the regime. An example of this is the daughters of Chávez, who live peacefully far from the Bolivarian revolution created by his father.

Rosinés Chávez, the youngest daughter with Marisabel Rodríguez, in 2017 went to Paris, with the excuse, to study at the University of La Soborna. The girl, according to some versions, spent 5 million Euros, in buying a luxurious 3-room apartment in Paris, near Trocadero Square, with a view of the Eiffel Tower.

The other daughter of the "Comandante", María Gabriela Chávez, lives very well in the American "empire". To justify his stay in the "empire", on August 13, 2014, Maduro appointed him as alternate ambassador of Venezuela to the UN. Some sources, they point out, that she has a fortune that exceeds 4 million dollars. Next to these two daughters of the "Commander", there is a son named Hugo Rafael, who also lives outside Venezuela, in luxury plan, thanks to the father's inheritance.

But they are not the only children, or relatives of Chavistas leaders who live far from the Bolivarian revolution. Interestingly, and I say curiously, since 2016, in Madrid, the Spanish capital, has experienced a boom in the sale of luxury apartment. I saw at the beginning of 2018, a couple of reports on Spanish television, where it was indicated, that those who lead the purchase of these apartments, are Venezuelans. And I told myself ... the Venezuelans ?. And there the bulb of the coconut lit up, remembering that since 2017, in Spain, a wave of what I would call, children of the Bolivarian revolution, that is, children, and relatives of Chavismo high offices, began to arrive, or high Chavismo officials with their families, who made their fortune with the so-called revolution, and who left Venezuela to enjoy life far from their revolution. These Chavistas are popularly known as Boliburgueses.

"Being rich is bad, it is inhuman. I say this, and I condemn the rich. " This statement is from Chávez in 2005. In that year, Venezuelan journalist Juan Carlos Zapata, coined the term boliburgués, to identify the bourgeois Bolivarians, already converted into millionaires, thanks to corruption, which according to Venezuelan parliamentary sources, is around 700 one billion dollars in 15 years.

Much of that money, has gone out of Venezuela, and a part, has gone to the purchase of luxury apartments in Madrid, or Barcelona.

So, if the Boliburgueses (wealthy Chavistas) escape their "revolution" abroad, what is left to other Venezuelans?.

Many of those "wealthy Chavistas" have chosen Spain as a place to live in the last decade. Also as a privileged destination of your investments. In September 2018, the Spanish newspaper El País published a report, which noted that a dozen people linked to Chavismo, have introduced more than 160 million euros in Spain in the last 15 years. Stresses that half of that money had been earmarked for real estate investments. It is estimated that only for Andorra, Chavismo high offices moved more than 2,000 million euros, as investigated by the justice of that country. A court in Houston (USA) has revealed the collection of tens of millions of euros in illegal commissions, then sent to Switzerland and tax havens. And a third investigation, launched by the Venezuelan government, quantifies in more than 10 billion dollars the corruption losses in the country, in the words of the Chavista attorney general, Tarek William Saab. Now, I imagine that if you ask Saab who took all that money, he will surely say that he has been people of the far right imperialist fascist. In short, according to the Chavista revolutionary ideology, no "revolutionary" leader is corrupt.

By the way, in mid-October 2018, Nervis Villalobos Cárdenas, who under Chávez's orders, had served as Deputy Minister of Electric Power between 2001 and 2006, is arrested in Madrid. Villalobos is accused by the Spanish justice system of washing of money. After his arrest, a court in Madrid has seized a luxury urbanization with more than 40 villas in Marbella (Málaga), as well as another hundred properties in other parts of Spain. Only in Madrid, had about 10 luxury apartments. That, only in Spain. Sure, that it will have something else in some other country, for example, Andorra, where it is also investigated for an alleged plunder of 2 billion dollars to PDVSA.

SOME CASES OF CORRUPTION

PDVSA is at the center of most cases of corruption, although the bribes extend to other projects such as the Caracas Metro, and the large investments made to face the electricity crisis suffered by Venezuela in 2009. To this end, the business is added with surcharges in the purchase of food, or medicines, with dollars granted to finger by the same government, to people linked to the chavismo, who then, after committing the scam, those leaders, or high Chavismo positions, grabbed the money , and they left to live far from the country. And a short time later, those foods, or medicines, that they had bought with surcharges, after arriving in the country, their destiny was to rot in abandoned containers in the ports of La Guaira or Puerto Cabello.

A small example is in the famous PDVAL case, related to the discovery of thousands of tons of food with expiration date expired in Venezuela in mid-2010, imported by the Chávez government under subsidies through the state company PDVAL (Producer and Distribuidora Venezolana de Alimentos), whose control, I insist, was totally in the hands of the Chavez government.

After exploding the scandal, three exgerentes were arrested, and then released, and to top it off, two of them reinstated in their positions. By the end of July 2010, official sources totaled 130 thousand tons of food affected, while the opposition gave a figure of 170 thousand tons. And the most striking thing in history, is that today, we do not know the results of the investigation that the National Assembly of Venezuela, under Chavez control at that time, had announced. In short ... nothing has happened, and millions of dollars went into the pockets of those who had set up the business with the importation of those expired foods.

By the way, there is an anecdote related to the case: It seems that, in June 2010, the government decided to send a boat with some 1,500 tons of food as a donation to Haiti. The issue is that the boat was returned by the government of the Dominican Republic, who organized the reception of humanitarian aid. The Dominican government alleged that the food was out of date. Three days later, the Venezuelan government denied this information, stating that "even though a ship with that amount of food had returned to Venezuela," it was under orders from the Venezuelan government, as it was considered that food would soon expire due to the existing conditions in Haiti. By the way, surely you will wonder, and in the end, where would those 1,500 tons of food go? I have researched a little, and I think, I have part of the answer. On July 17, 2010, Lara State Police in Venezuela arrested 43 people who were repackaging 68 tons of PDVAL milk, with an expiration date of November 29, 2009. The old milk bags were burned, while the milk was packaged in new bags under the legend "New Zealand pasteurized milk". The next day, the new president of PDVAL, Carlos Osorio, confirmed that this milk was being redistributed, but for animal consumption. PDVAL reported that more than 25 thousand tons of milk affected, were sold for this same purpose. However, the governor of Lara, Henri Falcón, questioned this explanation, assuring that the new packaging did not contain any clarification that indicated that the milk was not suitable for human consumption, and that it was not clear that it was for animal consumption. Anyway ... all this Show of PDVAL occurred in 2010, and today, there are many cases like PDVAL, where the Venezuelan citizen, before the brutal shortage, is poisoned every day, with products that they do not meet the minimum sanitary conditions. In fact, apart from the thousands of cases of malnutrition due to lack of food, this is compounded by the death of people "slowly poisoned" with expired or adulterated products. And before this reality, what is the position of the government? Well, there is no malnutrition, no deaths from hunger, or poisoning with expired or adulterated products that the same government supplies in the so-called CLAP bags.

Eye ... what happened with PDVAL, is small in front of the so-called Mission Mercal (Food Market). It was created in April 2003, and intended for the food sector, dependent on the Ministry of Food. It is a program that consists of building and providing warehouses and supermarkets with food and other basic necessities at low prices, so that they are accessible to the population most in need. The problem is that being something run by the Chavistas, well, corruption is at ease. For example, the idea of creating markets in the streets, to distribute food at low prices, has nothing to do with the reality of the Venezuelan who goes to these markets. The reality is that prices are inflated above the official price set by the government, and to top it off, many of those products, in the case of packaging, are already expired. A, and like the CLAP bags, many of the foods are destined to third parties, for example, "chavista" merchants who then resell them 60 or 70% more expensive on the street.

And we must not forget that during the first years of the revolution, Chávez confiscated some large supermarket chains in Venezuela, such as Cada, Éxito, or Bicentenario, where, after confiscation, the government injected millions of dollars, and to that in the end, with the bad management of the same government, they closed because they had stolen all the money. That yes, Chavistas friends who participated in the business, today are very happy. Why will it be?

Today, the few supermarkets and private chains, which have survived the revolution, have before them a future similar to the Cada, Éxito, or Bicentenario chains.

The revolution, to control, or rather, to destroy the food industry of the country, led to the idea that the best thing is to bring food containers from the outside. That is to say, today

Venezuela, more than 70% of the things that it consumes, are brought from outside, since as I have indicated previously, the same government has destroyed the productive apparatus of the country. Thus, it will be understood, that it is logical, that if a person goes to a supermarket in Caracas, it will be found that there are no fruits, meats, or basic products for personal cleaning. There are thousands of people, who for months, do not use a normal pill of soap, or toothpaste. Already for the Venezuelan, it is common, normal, not to brush your teeth, or not to shower and wash.

And is that perhaps, before the arrival of Chavismo to power, the country did not produce food or personal hygiene products ?. Well, no. The country produced what was necessary to supply its domestic consumption, and it was sold abroad. And when I lived in Caracas, there were a variety of brands of soap, toothpaste, colognes, perfumes, etc., that were produced in the country.

What Chavez has done since his arrival in power, well, is very simple. To give an example, in 2017, Kellogg's product companies, which had been in the country for more than 50 years, and had endured for 20 years all the manipulations, in the sense that the government itself was in charge of blocking the supplies of the raw material, in the end, had to leave the country, like other big companies, for example,, General Motors. And before this fact, what has the government done to this type of situation? Well, apply its great measure, which is to expropriate the facilities to the companies that announce the closure. And so, it has happened with hundreds of large companies, which have closed after the policy of blocking supplies, and then, the government announced, that as they have closed, they have had to confiscate them. The problem is that after confiscating, there is still a shortage of raw materials, the same or worse than ever. The unfortunate thing is that millions of dollars are destined from the government to refloat something, and where the government itself, as a manager, places people incapacitated professionally, for example, in PDVSA, and of course, the result is that in a few months , after wasting and stealing the money, they go bankrupt again. And then, the government says that the culprit is the "saboteurs", when the same government is the biggest saboteur.

Today, Venezuela, is a country where it is dangerous to be an entrepreneur, because the government considers them as enemies of the revolution. There is a Law of Costs and Prices that disables companies to make decisions. To this, other conditions are added, such as the existence of a currency exchange regime, which does not allow access to dollars to buy out the necessary inputs or services. There is also work rigidity that prevents being able to handle the work factor with freedom. A clear example of this rigidity, is that the government, when it sees that inflation continues uncontrolled, by decree, orders a salary increase, which, many of the companies, can not stand, and to top it off, the government decrees that nobody can be fired. In August 2018, Maduro decreed the minimum wage increase 35 times to its previous value accompanied by labor immobility. In short, Venezuelan businessmen live in an environment, where the highest is hyperinflation in the world, with the shortage of everything, and a lot of citizen insecurity, which makes many companies, make the most reasonable decision to close their doors . And if it closes, then Maduro arrives, and says "expropiese!".

By the way, I'm going to tell you a case. After the creation of the new Bolivar "sovereign" in August 2018, and the implementation of economic measures to "reactivate the country", a week later, the tire company Pirelli in Venezuela, temporarily closed its doors. The cause ... well, perhaps the fact that they have had problems with the supply of raw materials for years, which has led to the fact that their factories specialized in making tires for buses and motorcycles have been paralyzed for two years. Or perhaps the fact that since 2015, the Pirelli plant works at less than 50% of its capacity. Or maybe the fact that when they produced one million tires a year, by 2018 they have only produced 80,000. And before the problem, what has been the solution of the government ... Well, make a juicy business by bringing containers filled with Chinese tires, and that more than one chavista, as in the case of the CLAPS, have filled their pockets with dollars.

To give an example of the level of hallucination that one can find, in May 2018, arrived in Venezuela, a ship from Turkey, with more than 160 containers, out of a total of 368, planned in a commercial agreement between both governments. Apart from food and medicine, highlights tires and batteries for vehicles, which, most likely, and as has happened in other cases, then discover that they are not adaptable for vehicles circulating in Venezuela.

Maduro with his new ally the Turkish president Erdogan.

And you will wonder ... And because I'm talking about Turkey ... well, it's that of the other countries where expired products arrived, there are already problems, since the Venezuelan government has debts, and of course ... one day , Maduro wondered, what country with which I have no debts, could help me to strengthen my dictatorship ... and Turkey, emerged as a light at the end of the tunnel. The Turkish president Erdogan had revealed in May 2018 that the trade between Venezuela and Turkey had reached half a million dollars in the first months of 2018, and to top it off, he said he had faith that "this volume is going to reach a billion dollars by the end of the year." By the way, both presidents have certain similarities, in terms of pursuing media, or imprisoning opposition people.

In short, if Maduro has thousands of millions of debt with the Russians and Chinese, and no longer has oil to pay, what has he offered to the Turks? Anyway, I do not even want to imagine.

THE ECONOMIC MODEL CHAVISTA

As of March 2018, Maduro had announced that a new monetary cone would be implemented, where three zeros would be removed and the name of the currency would be changed to Bolívar Soberano. Then, in August of 2018, Maduro announces that there are no longer three zeros, but five zeros that will be removed. And to top it off, Maduro creates a supposed virtual currency called Petro, which, before being born, some economists announced their total fraud and failure.

By the way, the situation is so desperate for taking money from the dumbest, that at the end of August 2018, Maduro ordered the bank to adopt such cryptocurrency as the "unit of account". And to top it off, two months later, he announces that in November, the happy invisible coin will go on sale and that anyone could buy it. He had also announced that the few international airlines that arrive in Venezuela will have to pay for the fuel they require with Petros. And so, his intention is that everyone, instead of using dollars or euros, use their invisible currency.

The Petro, reminds me of my short visit to Cuba, back in 1999. During my stay at the airport in Havana, I was forced to buy some food in a cafeteria, where they only admitted dollars. After making the payment, as they had to return me money, they gave me some coins, which are only valid for the use of tourists inside Cuba, and which, according to the Cuban government, equals exactly the value with the dollar. The problem is that if I leave Cuba with those coins, they are not recognized in the rest of the world. With the Petro, Maduro wants to achieve something similar. Let's see if I explain. If an airline needs fuel, to pay in Petros, the government obliges it first to buy that "invisible currency", that is, to an official change that only the government itself puts, and very far from the reality of the market, if it is that there is a market to value a non-existent virtual currency. And what do you think what kind of currency the government will accept to sell those Petros to the airlines? Well, the blessed dollars or euros.

Maduro announcing the official creation of Petro.

Thus, Maduro, in his eagerness to surpass himself in inventing useless things to deceive people, with the happy Petro, is on track to surpass all the records. At the beginning of October 2018, he said that "the use of Petro as a unit of account is legalized as Venezuelan currency" and that local authorities will allow the sale of real estate, the payment of hotels, the purchase of international air tickets and the collection of exit taxes and other airport services, in the "cryptocurrency", which the government had allegedly put to market through six international exchange houses in the country.

Now, the idea of the Petro, its origin, I think, is somewhat controversial, if we take the background. Let's see, as of January 31, 2018, the Maduro government stated that it was totally legal to mine cryptocurrencies in Venezuela. Thus, for this purpose, a new bureaucratic office called superintendent of cryptoactives and related activities was created, popularly known as Superintendent of Cryptocurrencies. The Superintendent's name is Carlos Vargas, and in a statement at that time, the official had asserted that the use of the virtual currency is "totally legal" in Venezuelan territory, confirming that people who use Bitcoin and other cryptocurrencies would not be incurring in no act against the law. With this, to some extent, it was meant to imply that the Maduro government would have free hands to create its Petro, which by that time, was said to be designed with the backing of mineral reserves, and mainly of petrolium, with a token equivalent to 1 barrel of crude petroleum. So, to big plans, the government announced an initial offer of 100 million Petros, which supposedly would have a market value of approximately 6 billion dollars.

On February 23, 2018, the government began to deliver the "digital mining certificates" within hours of the presumed start of Petro's pre-sale. Subsequently, on April 9, 2018, thanks to a Decree of the Chavista National Constituent Assembly, all existence and creation of all cryptoactive, including Petro, was legalized.

And how has the evolution of the happy Petro been? In the month of August, Maduro said that with the sales of Petros, 3,300 million dollars had already been collected, and that the currency was being used to pay for imports. But Hugbel Roa, a cabinet minister involved in the project, had told a news agency that the technology behind the coin is still under development, and that "no one has been able to use the Petro". So, how Maduro has been able to sell 3,300 million dollars ?.

To top it off, at that time, Maduro announced that the salaries, pensions and exchange rate of Sovereign Bolivar would be linked to Petro. The question is that for many economists and experts in the field, they agree that "there is no way to link prices or exchange rates to a 'token' that is not marketed, precisely because there is no way of knowing how much sells really. "

As indicated above, the government had established the value of Petro at the price of a barrel of Venezuelan oil, which was backed by oil reserves located in an area of 380 square kilometers in the Atapirire area, which, according to the government, contains 5.3 One billion barrels of underground Petrolium.

For the ex-Minister of Petrolium of Chavez, Rafael Ramírez (now exiled), estimates that 20 billion dollars would be needed in investments to exploit Atapirire, money that PDVSA does not have. For the former minister, with the Petro "An arbitrary value is fixed, which only exists in the imagination of the government."

In short, with this, it demonstrates to some extent, the fraud character of the Petro, and more, when the Maduro regime falls into contradictions on the alleged sales of the "invisible currency". The funny thing is that as it is not sold, with arbitrary decrees, the government wants to impose the obligatory use of something that does not exist. In short, they are things that only happen in Venezuela.

Maduro announcing the creation of the sovereign Bolivar.

The creation of the new Bolivar Sovereign currency, and of

Petro, is as a consequence of the nefarious economic policies of the same government, which have led to hyper hyperinflation in Venezuela. To give an idea of the seriousness, already the International Monetary Fund (IMF), had announced in August 2018, that inflation in that country, for that year, would reach 1,000,000%. And after the entry into circulation of the so-called Sovereign Bolivar, new predictions have already come out of the IMF, that inflation in 2019 would be 10 million %. In short, as It would be said in my country Venezuela, the remedy has been worse than the disease.

In 2007, Hugo Chávez, faced with the same inflationary problem, had decided to remove three zeroes from the currency, and change the name of Bolívar, to Bolívar Fuerte (BsF). In 2018, Mr. Maduro, he believes, that by taking away another five zeros, the problem will disappear. But unlike in 2007, the Venezuela of 2018, is in a real economic and humanitarian chaos, where millions of Venezuelans, spend hardships, when it comes to getting food, or the most basic services.

By mid-2018, a worker earned a minimum salary of around BsF. 5 million per month (about $ 2.00 per change). Only a kilo of rice, at that time cost around 5 million Bs. So, with what he charges in a month's salary, he can not afford to live one day.

Another of the hardships experienced by Venezuelans is the ability to obtain food.

Since 2016, Venezuelans have changed their daily routine. People get up early to leave at 6 in the morning, to make a long queue in a market, without knowing, if when opening said trade at 8, there is some kind of food for sale. Moreover, these people spend 6 hours in the queue, and run the risk, that when their turn comes, there is no food. And if someone is lucky enough to get something, they will find that in the morning at 8 a person gets a kilo of rice at a price, and at morning 11 o'clock on the same day, the kilo of rice has already increased price up 10%.

When it comes to paying for the purchase, it's another mess. If you pay in cash, well, you had to have one, or two bags full of BsF. On the other hand, in the bank offices, there are no circulation mony. People could only withdraw 2 million BsF per day, so in order to buy a kilo of rice, a person had to go to the bank for three days to get enough money to be able to buy the product. And most striking, is that the bank gives users old bills of low denomination of 100 or 500 BsF., and the person leaves the bank with a bag full of paper money packages worthless.

The other option of the Venezuelan to make a purchase, is with the bank cards. The problem is that the merchants charge a juicy commission that reaches 25%.

So, that the Venezuelan on the street, is in a terrible situation when making any purchase. First: get up early and make long lines; second: to be lucky enough to get something to buy; third: to be lucky enough to have bags full of money for not paying with a card and to be charged additionally 25% of bank commission; and fifth, and most importantly, to be able to arrive alive at home, or not to be assaulted and robbed of the little food that he has been able to buy. And the tragedy of all this, is that this situation, that of the Venezuelan on the street, Mr. Maduro, knows it perfectly, since it is the same government, who controls all this mechanism, and Maduro believes, that by removing five zeros to the currency, and create a new "sovereign Bolivar", the problems will disappear.

The question is that with all this, what has happened, is that these problems have continued to get worse, and in less than a year, Maduro will surely say that we will have to take 6, or 10 zeros away from the currency, and create a new currency that could possibly be called super Bolívar, or super Petro.

In mid-2018, this whole mountain of money, was equivalent
to change a dollar bill on the black market.

Since the revolution came, in the currency market imposed by
the government, there are four or five changes of official currency against the US dollar, and all are controlled by the same
government, since unlike the rest of the countries, in Venezuela, the people, to get a dollar, have to go to a government
office, and justify and sign up on a list to ask for that foreign
currency. Problem, that this procedure before the government,
can last months, or years. For example, imagine that you are
an entrepreneur, and need dollars to buy some spare parts for a
machinery of your company. The reality is that many companies have had to close, because the government does not deliver
the necessary foreign currency to survive as a company. This
happens with the example of that company, it can be applied to
all sectors of the rest of the country. For example, already for
years, in hospitals there are no x-ray, dialysis, or other equipment, since the same government, has not been concerned
about maintaining them, or replace them with new equipment.
And if a person goes to a private clinic, the same thing happens.

In the case of private clinics, to acquire new equipment, they need dollars, and the dollars, can only be obtained through a government office, who a finger, decides, yes or no, being in the vast majority of cases, denied requests for currencies. Thus, the clinic closes, and then the government arrives and expropriates the facilities and equipments.

In 2015, my mother had a kidney problem. He went to a public hospital, and the doctor told him that they could not do the tests, because the devices there are damaged, so the doctor suggested that my mother go to a private clinic, and that she pay his analysis, and then, return with these results, for him, then give him a diagnosis. Imagine, that it was an emergency, and that in the hospital you needed to do those exams. The question is that the person would die, since in Venezuelan hospitals, there are not the minimum inputs needed to care for a person. This was in 2015 … imagine how it has worsened with the passage of time.

In mid-2016, I saw a report on Spanish television, where a journalist went to the university clinical hospital in Caracas. That hospital, in the 60s, was the most modern in Latin America in terms of facilities, and medical personnel. I saw, with disbelief, that the elevators did not work, and that to take a patient from the ground floor, or an upper floor, I saw how they had to improvise a stretcher, with a pieces of wood from a table, to place the patient, and take him between two people, up the stairs. I saw that, and almost I started crying.

Such is the poor health situation in Venezuela, that when Chavez fell ill in 2012, they had taken him to Cuba, to the socialist paradise of medicine.

And the Venezuelan, not only has to endure the chaos of hospitals. To this, it adds, that there are no drugs in pharmacies. Many companies in the sector have had to close, since the government does not give the necessary dollars to buy laboratory equipment or supplies for the manufacture of medicines. Many Venezuelans do authentic miracles, so that friends, or relatives who live outside the country, send them by mail, or with relatives who travel at a certain time. So that you have an idea of the gloom of the situation, for example, there are several international NGOs that make a great sacrifice to collect and send boxes of medicines to Venezuela, and when they arrive in the country, and go through the controls of Venezuelan customs, they are confiscated, by the Venezuelan authorities.

Since Chavismo came to power in Venezuela, they have always maintained that Cuban medicine is the best medicine in the world. Such is the extreme of ideological fanaticism, that Chávez, just taking power in 1999, signed an agreement with the island, to bring Cuban doctors to Venezuela. The Venezuelan Medical Federation, put the cry in the sky, since the government, was invading competitions, when wanting to supplant Venezuelan doctors by Cubans, who, without having done the legal procedures to practice the profession in Venezuela, could render their work without problems. And all this, thanks to the two governments, signed an agreement, where Venezuela offers tons of oil to the island, in exchange for doctors recently graduated in Cuba.

In recent years, the number of Cuban health workers in Venezuela had more than 30,000 members among doctors of various specialties, dentists, optometrists, physiotherapists and other technicians, according to official data.

The export of professional services, mainly medical, is the main source of foreign exchange for the island, and contributed between 2011 and 2015, an estimated annual average of 11,543 million dollars to Cuban coffers, according to official sources of the island . Most of that money, coming from Venezuela, in the form of oil.

By the way, there are Cuban doctors, who after having escaped from Venezuela to ask for asylum in a third country, have counted that, on instructions from Havana, they falsified by increasing income statistics and medical expenses far above. And with that, later the Cuban government issued invoices adulterated to the Venezuelan government. Thus, it is understood, how the island, makes medicine, its great lucrative business, being that, its main source of currency in dollars.

As an anecdote, I tell you something that could be said, it is the height of the highs. At the beginning of the year 2000, of the first batch of Cuban doctors who arrived in Venezuela, after stepping on Caracas, two of those doctors, Heberto Navarro and Reinaldo Calebrook, requested asylum in Venezuela. So the Chavez government found its first diplomatic crisis, since Venezuela was a friend of the Cuban revolution, and the idea of giving asylum to two Cubans, not fit very well. At that time, the Minister of Foreign Affairs of Venezuela, was José Vicente Rangel. The diplomatic problem was solved in a very curious way. Rangel proposed that these Cubans leave Venezuela and that they process their asylum application in a third country. Thus, the Venezuelan government was able to consolidate its good relationship with Cuba.

But that is not all. In that same year 2000, in Miami, eight Cuban doctors sued the governments of Cuba and Venezuela, and the state company PDVSA, for equivalent to slavery. So that they understand it better. If the Venezuelan doctors themselves work under infra human conditions, the Cubans would have to live their particular ordeal, suffering from lack of supplies, medicines, and working in totally unhealthy facilities.

The issue is that from the year 2000, and despite the threats of sanctions against their families on the island, many more Cuban doctors who arrived in Venezuela followed in the footsteps of Heberto Navarro and Reinaldo Calebrook. From the year 2000 to 2018, the exact or approximate figures of those who have requested asylum are unknown. It is known, for example, that from 2000 to 2006, some 500 Cuban doctors defected in Venezuela. The problem is that many of these Cuban doctors, knowing that Venezuela would deny them asylum, decide to risk leaving Venezuela for another third country, such as Colombia, from where they try to continue on their way to the US.. And is that many of them, after arriving in Colombia, or another third country, it is impossible to travel to the US, which is why they are left in an atypical illegal situation. That is to say, that Cuban doctor has a new problem before him, since it is not the same, to ask for asylum in Colombia, than in the USA. Thus, there are hundreds of Cuban doctors, who have escaped from Venezuela, divided by third countries, where they do not ask for asylum in that third country, waiting, to achieve their dream of treading Miami.

There is another very shocking reality about this whole history of Cuban doctors. The Venezuelan government pays Cuba, an average of about $ 4,000 for each doctor, while the Cuban government pays that doctor about $ 100.

By the way, not only doctors arrive from Cuba to Venezuela (about 30 thousand a year). There are also military (about 20 thousand a year).

Since the arrival of Chavez to power in Venezuela, there have been a variety of complaints about the penetration of Cuban military personnel within the Venezuelan Armed Forces, in areas that span the security and defense of the nation. And not only there the "occupation" of the Cubans arrived. For example, since 2015, there were Cuban personnel taking control of Social Security contributions in Venezuela. But in 2017, they left, since they could not stand the administrative chaos. To give an example of that chaos, for example, for a person to quote his monthly fee, he had to go every month to a bank office and fill out a form. The problem is that in the banks there are no such forms, since the government does not deliver them, with which, there are people who have six or seven months without making their payment, not because they do not have money, if not, because the same government system, it is chaos. And of course, Cuban officials see these anomalies, and prefer to leave that chaos in the hands of the Chavistas.

But not only Cubans have had access to the data of all Venezuelan contributors. They have gone much further. Already in 2003, Chávez signed an agreement with Cuba, for the issuance of official identity documents, in the deployment of the Identity Mission, which massified the issuance of identity cards in the months leading up to the 2004 recall referendum. And in 2014, Venezuela signed an agreement, where he put into Cuban hands, the design and management of a new Venezuelan civil identification system. That is, the Cuban government has a registry of all Venezuelans with their identity card numbers, or passport. Moreover, in Havana, they know that Venezuelans enter and leave the country, thanks to the strict control of passports.

Now, that agreement on identity issues, between the years 2009 to 2014, has represented the payment of Venezuela of about 1,400 million dollars to Cuba. I insist ... only on the agreement in terms of identity. And in the other areas, such as transport, security, food, etc., Cuba has taken another billions of dollars more. And everything, in return, that things have worsened. And a clear example of this is the issue of passports, or the management of strategic companies such as PDVSA.

At the end of July 2018, the leader of the Venezuelan opposition and coordinator of the Vente Venezuela movement, María Corina Machado, denounced that Fuerte Tiuna, the largest and most important Venezuelan military complex, which is the headquarters of the Army and the Ministry of Defense in Caracas, is full of Cubans, and also assured that 60% of Venezuelan territory is controlled by different paramilitary or guerrilla groups that "follow direct instructions from Havana, Cuba."

In short, you can not cover with a finger, the role of the Cuban regime, in terms of maintaining its ally Venezuela, which is the one that today supplies the dollars, and the necessary oil, to be able to survive.

WITH THE MILITARY THERE IS
MADURO FOR A LONG TIME

In 2018 Maduro was re-elected for the period 2019-2025, in the presidential elections. It is noteworthy that not only the Venezuelan opposition launched the cry to heaven condemning the Chavista dictatorship. Approximately 51 countries also joined the condemnation, highlighting organizations such as the OAS, the EU, the Lima Group and the Group of 7 (G7). All these countries, and international organizations, had stated that do not recognize Maduro as president, because that these elections of 2018 were illegal, and that they lacked minimum guarantees, and did not comply with the international standards of electoral processes.

On June 5, 2018, the OAS, with 19 votes in favor, 4 against and 11 abstentions, approved a resolution declaring illegitimate the re-election of Maduro and initiating the procedure to suspend Venezuela from the OAS. And to top it off, the president of Argentina, Mauricio Macri, had announced that he would denounce Maduro's government before the International Criminal Court (ICC) in The Hague for violations of human rights.

And to all this, what has Maduro said? Well, he does not care. He is still on his throne, and unfortunately, Venezuela is surpassing Cuba, in terms of lack of freedom, and suffering of its population.

There is a real fact, that many sometimes do not see. Maduro, endures in power, thanks to the regime has copied from Cuba, with a dictatorial model. And this, consists of the following:

After the arrival of Chávez to power, the first thing he did was a purge of the military commands. That is, forced the departure of those high officials who did not swear allegiance, then, be replaced, by others, who swore allegiance.

Then, militarized the high positions of the government and the companies of the state, as is the case of PDVSA.

In 2002, already Chávez, he had four military in his cabinet. In addition, PDVSA, and the industrial conglomerate of Corporación Venezolana de Guayana, are also run by men-at-arms. At least fifty military in that year 2002, occupied middle ranks in the government, the diplomatic service, and state companies.

By the end of 2017, of the 29 cabinet ministers, 10 are military or former military, and the number of military officers in companies occupying positions, the exact figure is unknown, but the safest thing is that it is much higher than the figures of the year 2002.

Military high command in 2019, headed by Vladimir Padrino, in one of his many official statements, announcing his full support to Maduro.

Despite the fact that the armed forces must be apolitical, according to the 1999 Constitution, Maduro's defense minister, Vladimir Padrino, closes his official statements: "Chávez lives, the country continues, Independence and socialist homeland."

Come, that not even in the communist Cuba, I believe, that the defense minister of that country closes its communiqués with a similar phrase.

The current support of the Maduro government has undoubtedly been the military, converted not only into political actors, but also into businessmen, who control the most important sectors of the economy. Under President Chávez, the military had carried out activities in the economic sector, such as the Bolivar 2000 Plan for the distribution of food, and even the presidency of PDVSA. However, with Maduro, the role of the military became predominant, given that active and retired personnel were given control over the electricity sector, the Caracas metro, the aluminum, iron and steel companies in the south of the country, as well as ports and customs.

As of 2013, four military companies were formed: the Bolivarian National Armed Forces Bank (BANFANB), a television channel (TVFANB), a company for the transport of cargo by air, sea and land called EMILTRA, and the company agricultural AGRO-FANB. And in 2016, faced with the growing economic crisis, the control process of the military sector expanded to strategic areas, such as food and extractive resources.

Faced with the serious problems of shortages of food and medicines, as well as other basic health and education services, the regime decided to establish in August 2016 the Grand Mission Sovereign and Secure Supply, under the command of the Minister for Defense, a military active. In this framework, 18 generals were appointed who would be in charge of purchasing / importing and distributing the food and medicine items considered a priority. It should be noted that since 2004, of the 11 food ministers, 10 had been military. However, despite military control, the situation of shortages of food and medicines was continuously deepened. There is no access to official data, but at the beginning of 2018 the experts calculated that the shortage of food was around 80%.

Although it did not show any capacity to face these basic problems, the Maduro government gave the military sector a greater presence in the strategic areas of the country. On February 10, 2016, the Military anonymous company of mining, oil and gas industries (CAMIMPEG), was established, which signed several memoranda of understanding with PDVSA. It was also granted an important role in the Orinoco Mining Arc, which according to the government, seeks to overcome the "oil rentiery" and diversify its activity towards mining, focused on the exploitation of, gold, diamonds and coltan.

On November 26, 2017, the military power over the Venezuelan economy was consolidated with the appointment of a General of the GNB, without any experience in the area, as president of PDVSA and, simultaneously, as Minister of Energy. In this way, the military elite came to dominate the most important sector of the economy, which contributes more than 95% of the income of the national budget.

At least 785 active and retired officers, have directed companies that had contracts with the government in areas of construction, importation of medicine and food, as well as supplies for the health sector, among others. Perhaps, that is why it would be understood, why the military, or rather, the military high command, is to death with Maduro.

A, one thing that Chávez and Maduro copied from the Cuban regime, is the incentive for many of those high-ranking military officers, put in those positions to finger by the supreme commander, to do in the name of the government, big illicit businesses with dollars , with which, without a doubt, corruption has been a factor, which has helped to sustain Chavism in Venezuela. That is to say, today Maduro remains in power thanks to that corruption, because if one day Maduro falls, the most feasible thing is that those military would also fall with him.

So, for those who still have the idea, or illusion, that the military can one day get Maduro out, well, forget about the idea. As I see the panorama, there is Maduro for a while!

THE EXPROPRIATION BUSINESS
AND THE RABBIT PLAN

A few years ago, a friend of Spanish origin in Madrid, had asked me, where I could buy Venezuelan coffee. And I answered him that if in Venezuela, today there is no coffee, it would be very difficult to get it in Madrid. And how is it possible that one of the best coffee producers in the world, today, its population, at best, consumes Brazilian or Nicaraguan coffee? The answer is very simple: In 20 years of Chavez revolution, the government destroyed agricultural production.

I insist ... the government assumed the role of ruining the large, medium, and small producers, denying them all kinds of economic aid for supplies, or raw materials, and then, after leaving those companies in ruins, he devoted himself to confiscate land and companies. And thanks to that, the country stopped producing. Thus, in order to satisfy the internal demand for coffee consumption, or other products, the government does its business by bringing its containers from Brazil or Nicaragua. That if, paying always with surcharges, to share more dollars between his cronies Chavistas "businessmen".

In 2009, Chávez expropriated the country's two main coffee producers, Fama de América and Café Madrid, which, before their confiscation, processed 62% of the coffee produced in Venezuela. Since then, the freezing of the price of coffee, and the shortage of fertilizers, insecticides and seeds, have helped cause the ruin of the coffee farmers, who must also sell the harvest at the same cost of their production, which did not generate them profits to invest in their industry, not to mention the consequences on incentives. And what has been the result of the Chavista policy ?: The coffee industry has fallen by 94%, compared to 1998, when Venezuela managed to not only meet the domestic demand for coffee, but also export 600,000 quintals each year.

As the shortage of food of agricultural origin worsened, already in 2010, Chavez began to campaign for the people of the big cities to cultivate in their homes. I remember that at the beginning of 2011, the "commander" had the idea of saying that he has a small garden where he grew products in the presidential palace. The idea of urban agriculture was copied from Cuba, a country that has been accustomed to that life for 50 years under communism, and where what is produced, for the most part, is for the government itself.

Venezuela today has some 30 million hectares of crops, and by 2012, the government had expropriated four million hectares, with the excuse, to boost the sector. The issue is that with the so-called "Bolivarian revolution", what has been achieved is that farmers stopped producing. And faced with the shortage and inability of the government to generate crops, Chávez came up with the idea of copying the Cuban agricultural model. That is, it takes away the land from the producers, to make it unproductive, and in the face of a shortage of food, the "commander" then told the people, so that they would not go hungry, As the shortage of food of agricultural origin worsened, already in 2010, Chavez began to campaign for the people of the big cities to cultivate in their homes. I remember that at the beginning of 2011, the "commander" had the idea of saying that he has a small garden where he grew products in the presidential palace. The question is that the idea of urban agriculture was copied from Cuba, a country that has been accustomed to that life for 50 years under communism, and where what is produced, for the most part, is for the government itself.

Venezuela today has some 30 million hectares of crops, and by 2012, the government had expropriated four million hectares, with the excuse, to boost the sector. The issue is that with the so-called "Bolivarian revolution", what has been achieved is that farmers stopped producing. And faced with the shortage and inability of the government to generate crops, Chávez came up with the idea of copying the Cuban agricultural model. That is, it takes away the land from the producers, to make it unproductive, and in the face of a shortage of food, the "commander" then told the people, so that they would not go hungry, that producen food in their own home.

One of those vertical chicken coops built on a concrete planter in the center of Caracas.

A, and we must not forget, that in 2010, Chávez, proposed something called "vertical chicken coops". That is, raise chickens inside your house. The issue is that raising chickens, involves some health risks, because when dealing with animals, can cause diseases that can infect humans. In short, anyone who wants to have one of those vertical chicken coops in their house, the minimum to make it work, should have regular health inspection with a veterinarian that controls the health of the animals, and also need vaccines, vitamins, minerals from the animal , and an adequate feeding for the hens. And to this day, how many vertical chicken coops are there in Venezuela? All I know is that both Chávez, and later Maduro, allocated money to create those chicken coops. And as always, the result is that there are no chicken coops, and the money has been stolen away by some friends of the revolution.

A ... and before the lack of meat, well ... the Chavistas have some ideas, come on, that if it is not to cry, you laugh a lot. In 2017, Maduro, in a broadcast national of the radio and television, came up with the idea that, since there are problems with meat supply in the country, there are people who, at home, have rabbits as pets, and that these rabbits can be consumed.

So, he recommended that people eat their pets, or rather, their rabbits. Most likely, is that when things get put worse, Maduro will say that in China, people eat dog meat, and that in Venezuela, there are many people who have pet dogs.

The Minister of Urban Agriculture, Freddy Bernal.

The truth is that for this nonsense, Maduro had created a ministry of urban agriculture, and thus, justify the new spending of millions of dollars on these new projects totally unviable. In short, as I have indicated, one more way to steal and deceive the citizen.

Caricature published in the newspaper El Nacional de Venezuela, glimpsing the possible future food plans of the Government of Maduro.

After Maduro's idea to eat their pets, the Minister of Urban Agriculture, Freddy Bernal, decided to launch the "rabbit plan". That is to say, a copy of the vertical chicken plan, but they simply change the character's name, and that if, spending more money that is lost, without clear results. And what did the minister say to justify the rabbit plan? Well, as it is an animal species with high fertility, the idea would be to distribute pairs of animals to different communities, with the hope that these begin to reproduce, well, "just like rabbits." According to the minister "a rabbit produc approximately ten or twelve bunnies, in the end eight are raised. In two and a half months we have a rabbit weighing two and a half kilos. " According to the minister's calculations, each rabbit could be producing around 80 bunnies a year, which, in turn, would soon have a multiplier effect in the country.

The minister sees only one small problem in the plan: "There is a cultural problem, which has taught us that the rabbit is a very beautiful pet. And without a doubt that the rabbit is a beautiful animal, it is true, but the rabbit could be a solution".

According to the minister "We have to have a campaign of radio, press, television, cartoons, everywhere so that the people understand that the rabbit is not a pet, but they are two and a half kilos of meat, with high protein and without cholesterol, put on the table of the Venezuelan ".

In short, and to all this of the vertical chicken coops, and the rabbit plan, which the minister of health said? Well, nothing. Now, do you imagine the big health problem that would generate in the cities to raise chickens and rabbits in unhealthy conditions ?.

As day of today, I have not seen official figures of the results of the vertical chicken coops plan, or the rabbitsplan. It is unknown how many millions of dollars were spent, and how many chickens, eggs, or rabbits were produced.

The cruel reality of the country, before the authentic disaster of destruction developed by Chavismo in the different productive means, is taking the country to an authentic humanitarian tragedy. And it is not because it does not rain, there are droughts, or there are no lands to cultivate and produce cattle. I insist ... the problem is Chavismo.

The truth is that for years, the Venezuelan is enduring, what some call "the Maduro diet." And you will wonder what is that ?. Well, so that you have an idea of what it is, I will give you a datum: According to the Survey of Living Conditions (Encovi), "74% of Venezuelans have lost an average of 8.7 kilos in weight (almost 20 pounds) during the year 2017, while 32.5% of Venezuelans, including children and the elderly, eat two or less times a day ". That's the "Maduro diet."

In short ... the Chavista regime, after ruining and expropriating, has lands, supermarket chains, sets prices, and then, in the face of food shortages, produced by the policies of the same regime, sends you to plant on your terrace, raise chickens, or rabbits.

With Chavez, the oil barrel was 100 dollars, and he imported coffee from Brazil, Caraotas from the Dominican Republic, rice from Nicaragua. When Maduro arrived, and the low barrel at 50 dollars, it was no longer profitable to import, and for 15 years, it had not been produced in the country. This is the reason that has given rise to the great shortage of food, and the famine in the country.

THE ROLE OF PARTIES OF OP-
POSITION IN VENEZUELA

I believe that, without doubt, the Venezuelan opposition to the Chavez regime has a large share of responsibility, given the great chaos that has arrived in the country.

I could say, that Chavismo, since its inception, has applied a well-known strategy, which consists, in dividing your opponent, and you will win. And since Chávez's victory in 1998, the opposition has always been divided, since many of its leaders prefer to defend their personal positions, and not join their possible ideological allies, and face a common enemy, with a common project of future. I insist ... throughout 20 years, they have only faced the enemy, without a common project with future viability. That is, there is an idea that is to get out of chavismo. The problem is that there is no serious plan to rebuild the country after the Chavismo exit. In short and to be very clear: Today we leave Chavismo, and tomorrow we see what we do or invent.

Demonstrations, strikes, accusations of fraud, have been the strategy of the opposition in more than 20 years, and nonetheless, the Chavismo, continue stronger in power.

In 2002, the opposition was grouped in the so-called Democratic Coordinator. In 2004, that Coordinator focused all its efforts so that the so-called recall referendum could be called. To do this, the Chavez government, at all times, set the guidelines and conditions for the referendum to take place. One of those conditions is that the opposition would have to submit some forms, with names, document number, signature, and fingerprint. In spite of the various complaints made by the government during the process of collecting signatures, and after overcoming the various obstacles, they finally presented the final list with millions of data of people, which in the end, the government itself, would use, for Create a blacklist (Tascón list). And to top it off, the opposition allows the government to mount alone, its referendum, where, as is logical, Chávez won.

This was the first failure of the opposition, and as a result, the Democratic Coordinator was dissolved.

In 2006, the opposition to the challenge of the presidential elections of that year, join in the so-called National Unity, to offer a single candidate against Chavez, and that only candidate named Manuel Rosales, ultimately lost.

In 2007, the National Unity makes a strong campaign of the No against the constitutional reform promoted by Chávez, obtaining the opposition, a temporary triumph.

Act of official presentation of the Broad Front in 2006.

After this triumph, the name is changed to Democratic Unity Table (MUD), which was formed by 18 different political parties, ranging from the center right, to the extreme left. So, it will be understood that sitting all those people at the same table, sounds impossible, since each one proposes a different vision, of how to get out of chavism. In fact, some of the leaders of those parties, questioned the decisions of one, or another, and one could say, that there was a kind of internal war.

Despite winning the No in the referendum of 2007, the same day of the results, Chávez announced that he would try again, and the result was that the following year, the "commander" achieved his desired constitutional reform. Unlike the reform rejected in year 2007, the of is from 2008, it was more extreme. In short, another defeat for the opposition, which participated in a second referendum on constitutional reform, which they themselves had said a year before it was illegal.

Members of the MUD in 2007.

With these two examples, the 2004 recall referendum and the constitutional reform of 2007-2008, it can be perfectly understood why the Venezuelan opposition is considered by some to be the support of Chavez.

The Chávez government has known all along how to manipulate the opposition. First, creating an electoral system, where sometimes, the opposition goes to the elections or not. That same opposition, has made allegations of fraud, which in the end, have come to nothing. In short, the government has fun seeing how their opponents fight each other, and do not know how to do things well.

In all these years, the opposition has set the goal of getting out of chavismo, but the issue is that they do not explain what kind of country they want after chavismo, and how the charges would be divided between 18 or 25 different parties. They do not fix a clear strategy, a contingency plan, or even worse, they do not convince society, since they are practically lurching from one side to the other. In short, if you ask the opposition leaders what they would do after Maduro left, surely the answer would be that they have no idea. Among the internal conflicts that exist within the MUD, and the measures taken by the government of Maduro every day, the truth is that the opposition has not been able to take a clear strategy.

If from the first elections they already knew that the electoral system with electronic vote was a fraud, why in all these 20 years the political opposition they have participated in these false elections?

I insist, unfortunately the political opposition, does not have a clear and concise plan of how to get Maduro out of power, and which is the Venezuela that we are going to build after the fall of Chavismo.

Another aspect to highlight is that when there is an opposition leader, who demonstrates certain serious threat criteria to replace Chávez or Maduro, the government has taken its measures. And you will wonder what these measures have been ... Well, very simple: persecute, arrest, disqualify, judicially, or put in jail, those opposition leaders. Cases like those of Juan Requesens, Leopoldo Lopez, Antonio Ledezma, Freddy Guevara, are a small example of what happens in the country. The opposition speaks of political prisoners, and the government of confessed criminals. The issue is that not even the opposition, is able to some extent, to defend their leaders imprisoned or politically disabled, as are the cases of Enrique Capriles, or María Corina Machado. Both have been disqualified from running or holding public office. Much fuss at first, but then, it seems that they forget about the subject.

By the way, after the presidential elections of 2018, the opposition was divided into three groups: MUD, Frente Venezuela, and Concertación por el Cambio. And Maduro, very happy about that.

All this reminds me, when at the beginning of the 60s, the Cuban opposition announced every day, that Fidel Castro would not hold another day in power. And 60 years have passed, and Castroism is still intact in power. I do not want to be pessimistic, but Venezuela is going the same way, and within 60 years, many Venezuelan opponents will continue to say that Chavismo is about to fall. In fact, they have been saying it for almost 20 years.

I think that the solution is for the MUD, and the rest of the opposition, to carry out a profound renovation of their leaders, since, for 20 years, they have been almost the same leaders who have led, in some measure to the country, to where we are today, with a Maduro as president.

In January 2019, one sector, the opposition, understood that a new figure or leader had to be supported, and that leader was Juan Guaidó, who after being appointed president of the parliament, assumed by constitutional means the position of president in charge of Venezuela. In a chapter later, I will tell you the story of Guiadó's arrival.

In short, the solution in Venezuela is not just to leave Maduro. The solution is for the opposition to know how to create a real alternative for the reconstruction of the country, after the departure of Maduro, and of all the Chavistas of all the State institutions (mayorships, governorships, judicial power, etc.).

Juan Guaidó, the new Venezuelan opposition leader.

The solution to the Venezuelan crisis, is not is put an interim president (without real powers) as Guaidó, and call new clean elections, with international support. The political opposition has to demonstrate that they have concrete and real plans, of how the country is going to be rebuilt, how to rebuild and create new companies, how to recover the hospitals, agricultural infrastructure, etc. I have seen, with some disbelief, that some opposition leaders are announcing, with a lot of joy, that the International Monetary Fund is going to offer money. I insist, Venezuela plus what it needs, is to have clear and concrete plans, how to know how to use that money for its reconstruction, without forgetting, that they have to have a team of serious professionals, capable of putting these plans to work. It is very nice to say that they are going to rebuild and equip all the hospitals. But from what has been said, to the fact, there is a great path. So, I think that if the opposition wants to be taken seriously, the first thing they have to do is demonstrate, that they have work teams, with professionals with recognized capacity, and willing to take on the job of rebuilding a country.

THE INTERNATIONAL COMMUN-
ITY IN FRONT OF MADURO

Many make a comparison of Venezuela, with what lived in Cuba in the 60s, after the Castro revolution, where more than a million Cubans, left with nothing and in rafts floating, risking their lives, crossing waters full of sharks, with the dream of arriving in the USA

Venezuela is experiencing a similar process, and regrettably, institutions such as the OAS, or the UN, have not taken serious and direct measures to defend the right of all those Venezuelans who have left their country, against their will. Of course, many foreign leaders give nice speeches condemning chavism, but unfortunately, they are just beautiful speeches, which do not help in solving the reality of Venezuela.

Thousands of Venezuelan refugees cross a border post to Colombia.

For his part, Maduro, is very happy, because for him, those people who leave the country, is a problem less for him, and a problem for the other countries, which have to face in their hands a very serious situation , which is to attend, feed, give medical health care, to all that human mass that escapes the Bolivarian revolution. None of the affected countries wants to call the problem by its name, which is a wave of refugees. If they are recognized as refugees, there, if the OAS and the UN, they would have to assume their humanitarian work by having to set up camps and send specialized personnel with supplies of medicines and food in order to adequately attend to these "refugees". But it seems that these organizations, prefer to look the other way, and let each affected country, take their own initiatives each by their side.

It is curious, for example, that in March 2018, the UN Agency for Refugees (UNHCR) cataloged "officially" the Venezuelan migrants as refugees, for which, said organization "urges the receiving states and / or those that already welcome Venezuelans to allow them access to their territory and to continue adopting adequate and pragmatic responses oriented to protection and based on good practices existing in the region." But unfortunately the reality is different.

Thus we find, for example, that Peru, in mid-August 2018, had more than 100 thousand requests from Venezuelans to enter the country as refugees. And what has been the response of said government? Put in force a rule that requires them to present their passport in order to access their territory. That is, the Peruvian government, knowing in advance that the Maduro government does not grant passports, believes that the solution to the Venezuelan genocide is not to let people who do not have a passport enter. The example of Peru, we can see it in Brazil, Ecuador, or Panama. With what I mean, is that many countries in the region, see that there is a serious problem in a brother country, and instead, to ask or agree on a clear solution to end the Maduro regime, believe that by blocking the borders, the Venezuelans will live happier.

The Secretary General of the OAS Luis Almagro.

The Secretary General of the OAS, Luis Almagro, in mid-September 2018, said that a military intervention to Venezuela should not be ruled out as an alternative to overcome the political and economic situation of the country. Almagro, even on behalf of the OAS, had pointed out that the "regime" of Nicolás Maduro, "is perpetrating crimes against humanity and violation of Human Rights." And to top it off, the top leader of the OAS, noted that before thinking of a military intervention, "diplomatic actions are in first place." And I'm wondering ... for more than 15 years there has been talk of diplomatic actions and international mediation for Venezuela, and the reality is that Maduro, is getting stronger every day in his presidential chair.

So, it seems, that the secretary general of the OAS, has not heard, that for years, the Venezuelan opposition, has come to diversity of international organizations (OAS, UN, EU, MERCOSUR, Parlatino, etc.) to ask a solution, and the mediation of those organizations, and I insist, the only thing that the opposition has achieved, are beautiful speeches from all those international organizations, condemning the Chavista dictatorship. And while, both Chavez and Maduro, they have followed doing what they want, and do not care, what the international community says. To do this, the chavistas they have created what some call the new "axis of evil", that is, a group of countries allied with the Chavista regime, such as Russia, China, North Korea, Turkey, Cuba, Nicaragua, El Salvador, Bolivia, and Ecuador. And all those countries have something in common: Maduro gives them Petroleum.

A final attempt at a dialogue of international agreement to seek a solution to the Venezuelan case in 2018 was in the Dominican Republic. In January of that year, and after two different attempts at negotiations in December 2017 without agreements in Santo Domingo, a last effort was made for this so-called dialogue. One of the issues under discussion on the table was the illegal and fraudulent convocation by Maduro of a presidential election without democratic guarantees. After the negotiations, Dominican President Danilo Medina presented a draft agreement between the parties (government and opposition). And in the end what happened in that supposed negotiation ?. Well, the representatives of the Chavista government, refused to sign the document. Moreover, later, Maduro in Caracas, made his own version of the document called "peace agreement", of course, with its conditions, which, in the end, he only signed alone. That is, unilaterally, he leaves the dialogue table in Santo Domingo, and then says that there is already a "peace agreement" that the opposition refuses to sign in Caracas. And I wonder ... and the pre-agreement document presented by the Dominican president, after supposedly three months of negotiation, what was that for?. In the end, Maduro did what he wanted, and does only in Caracas do his particular and unilateral version of what he calls "agreement of peace".

And before this international joke on the part of the chavista regime, even Almagro says that before thinking about a military intervention, "the diplomatic actions are in first place".

The Dominican President Medina, accompanied by his foreign minister, Vargas, and the negotiator sent by Maduro, the spanin Rodríguez Zapatero.

The Chavista regime is not interested in reaching agreements with the leaders of the opposition. The regime, from its first day (more than 20 years ago), maintains its biased and monolithic vision of its reality, in which it states, that in the country there are no political prisoners, or that people do not go hungry and there no misery. The regime has only been dedicated to consolidate its international image paying with Petrodollars to "friends" with ideological tendencies of the international left, to focus its own campaign of victimhood.

A clear example of this, we can see it with a former president of the Spanish government, the socialist José Luis Rodríguez Zapatero, who has been dedicated for some time, as an "international mediator" paid by Maduro in Venezuela. And that, I did not say it! It is affirmed by all the Venezuelan opposition.

Visit of Zapatero to Maduro in Caracas in May 2018.

In May 2018, Zapatero was invited by Maduro as an international observer in the elections that the entire international community condemned as fraudulent, while Zapatero, it seems that he did not see any fraud. To see the cynicism of Zapatero in defense of Maduro, in mid-September 2018, in one of his many visits to Caracas, it occurred to him to say, that the exodus of more than two million people escaping from the Chavez regime is caused by US economic sanctions. That is to say, Mr. Zapatero implies that in Venezuela, an authentic democracy is lived, and that the fault lies with the American empire. One curious thing about his activity as mediator, is that every time he travels to Venezuela, he only meets with Maduro, while the opposition, for some time, has closed the doors. So, we have a supposed "mediator" who has only dedicated himself to defending the image of the regime. To the list of international characters, paid for by Chavismo, we have, for example, the soccer player Diego Armando Maradona. And there are those who say that Pope Francis himself is on the list. Perhaps it is because of the fact that he has never condemned the Maduro regime.

VENEZUELA: TWO PRESIDENTS

In one of my previous chapters, I had told you about the May 2018 elections, where Maduro was "auto" elected. The vast majority of the international community condemned these elections as fraudulent.

Since the end of May 2018, the Venezuelan opposition raised a plan, to look from the constitutional point of view, that is, using the same constitution created by the chavistas to finger, a legal way to delegitimize Maduro as president-elect in those fraudulent elections.

Maduro swears before the Constituent Assembly on May 24, 2018

One of those legal channels is that Maduro should have assumed the post on January 10, 2019 before the National Assembly of Venezuela (NAV), today, with an majority of opposition partys deputies. As Maduro does not recognize that Assembly, he created his version of a parallel Parliament called the Constituent Assembly (CA), which has the particularity that 100% of its members are Chavistas. Thus, according to Maduro, he could assume the presidency, only by swearing in his Assembly. Thus, that on May 24, 2018, and in against the Chavez Constitution, he was sworn in to the CA.

On the other hand, before the warnings issued by the opposition about Maduro's unconstitutional oath, the Chavistas, to supposedly clear up any possible doubts of illegality, decide to swear on January 10, 2019, before the Supreme Court of Justice (CSJ). , organ, in which 100% of its members, were put to finger by the same Maduro.

On January 10, 2019, Maduro swears in before the Supreme Court of Justice.

Thus, on January 10, 2019, the legal deadline established for swearing in the NAV, Maduro set up another show, and is sworn in by the TSJ, thereby violating the Venezuelan Constitution for the second time, for not swearing in as president-elect before the NAV.

And before this panorama of illegitimate double oath of Maduro, what has the opposition done? As I have indicated previously, since the end of May 2018, the opposition already raised the idea of not recognizing Maduro. In fact, the NAV agreed to name him as "usurper" of the post, because it did not meet the minimum democratic conditions, and for violating the Constitution.

On the other hand, and as a result of this constitutional violation, it was legally stated that after January 10, a vacancy would be established in the office of the presidency, with which, who would have to assume the position temporarily, and until call new elections, would be the president of the NAV.

Thus, the NAV, in a pre-established agreement, had agreed that at the beginning of January, they would elect a new board of directors, with the deputy Juan Gerardo Guaidó Márquez appointed as President, formally assuming this position on January 5, 2019, being the Younger person to assume that responsibility in the history of Venezuela.

Subsequently, on January 23, 2019, in a multitudinous act in Caracas called Cabildo Abierto, the majority of the NAV, agrees to swear in Guaidó, as president in charge of Venezuela, temporarily, until the convocation of new elections, assuming constitutionally said charge, based on article 233.

Guaidó, during the act of appointment as
president in charge of Venezuela.

That same day 23, several countries, including the US, recognize him in office. Venezuela, has an two presidents: One, illegitimate (Maduro), violating the chavista Constitution and laws election; and another president (Guaidó), who assumes the position temporarily, according to that Constitution.

Thus, Maduro, outside of Venezuela, has only the support of China, Russia, Nicaragua, Bolivia, Uruguay, Mexico, and Turkey. It is noteworthy that all these countries, especially China, Russia and Turkey, are not interested in Maduro leaving, because thanks to him, Venezuela has a debt of billions of dollars with these countries.

As for Guaidó, despite many acknowledgments from governments of other countries as president in charge of Venezuela, the problem is that who has control of the country, or rather, who decides whether Maduro whether or not he leaves the position of president, is the high corrupt cupola of the Venezuelan army.

As I pointed out in a previous chapter, Chavismo mounted an infrastructure of power where corruption in the army has made those generals, admirals, colonels, etc., faithful to the regime that fills their pockets with dollars. Thus, the opposition, knowing perfectly the problem, has glimpsed the idea of approving in the NAV a "supposed" amnesty law, addressed in a special way, to those military and civilians who decide to stop supporting Maduro, and to "collaborate in the restitution of the constitutional order in Venezuela."

In said law, there is a section focused on eliminating the "civil, criminal, administrative, disciplinary and tax liability of investigations, proceedings, penalties or sanctions" from January 1, 1999, one month before Chávez takes office. That is, the law, in principle, is intended for "all civilians, military and other officials identified as prisoners, persecuted and political exiles for acts committed from January 1, 1999 until the entry into force of this law." This would imply the immediate release from prison of many of the opponents who remain in jail. So far, you can understand the positive side of that law.

But this supposed law has its contradictory part. It states that "All constitutional guarantees shall be granted in favor of all those civil and military officials who, acting on the basis of articles 333 and 350 of the Constitution of the Bolivarian Republic of Venezuela, cooperate in the restoration of democracy and the constitutional order in Venezuela, violated by the de facto regime led by who today is usurping the Presidency of the Republic". That is to say, it can be interpreted that the civilian or military man responsible for plundering millions of dollars, if he decides to go against Maduro, is forgiven. In other words, it is looking in a somewhat illicit way, to forgive war criminals, and even worse, to continue to enjoy their high positions, and everything in exchange for stopping supporting Maduro.

Faced with this supposed amnesty law, I believe that the opposition has made a mistake in trying to "clean up" the military high command. I think that those high military or civilian Chavistas officials, with their bank accounts full of dollars in tax havens, with houses, cars, and privileges, are not so stupid to leave Maduro. These people are very clear, that if one day Maduro falls, all of them, to some extent, would fall, since it is such a level of responsibility, that it is unforgivable, to give an amnesty to someone who has used his position to literally kill thousands of people of hunger and misery. A, and we must not forget the thousands of cases of human rights violations, with torture, persecution, or murder of innocents in 20 years of chavismo. I only mention one case: On the same day, January 23, 2019, during the opposition demonstrations, only that day, it is estimated that more than 40 people were murdered. And I ask myself: How is it that the opposition proposes an amnesty law for Chavistas criminals?

I insist, the fact of the Chavismo leaders during 20 years of "revolution" have made lucrative illicit businesses, thanks to playing with the misery of a country, has no forgiveness. Nor should those responsible for ordering and violently repressing peaceful opposition demonstrations and shooting, injuring and killing innocent people be pardoned. And if the future new government, raises the "give a forgiveness" to those responsible (direct or indirect), I think, we will have learned nothing of this history. It is as if after the defeat of Germany in World War II, the allied powers forgive all the Nazi criminals, responsible for millions of deaths.

I think that what the future new government would have to propose is a law of justice, where it is clearly stated, that everyone who has profited illegally, criminally, using the excuse of the "revolution", will have its corresponding sanction , either, with jail, community work, confiscation of goods resulting from a crime, etc. And the most important thing: Anyone who is directly, or indirectly, responsible for torture, murder, kidnapping, or similar acts, will be tried in an international court of justice, so that later, do not say that the Venezuelan judicial system is still contaminated by Chavismo.

Believe me, that if the opposition assumes that role of settling accounts with the Chavistas criminals, and that those criminals serve life sentences in prisons outside of Venezuela, for example, in Brazil, or Colombia, surely those high-ranking military officers who support Maduro today , I insist, they would surely grab their suitcases full of dollars and go to countries where there is no extradition. I insist ... with this type of ads, even Maduro himself, he would have fled the country.

But that the Venezuelan opposition wants to play that nothing has happened in Venezuela, and nobody is guilty, it is not what the countrydeserves. And more, when there are sectors from the opposition, which clearly speak of giving an amnesty to Nicolás Maduro himself.

Fernando Germán M

I insist ... I believe that the international community has to take measures to create a real transition in Venezuela, that is, without creating amnesty laws for Chavistas criminals.

In the next chapter, I will comment, from my point of view, what would be the solution to the case of Venezuela.

MY VISION OF THE SOLUTION
TO THE CASE VENEZUELA

And after telling all this long story, how Nicolás Maduro, and Chavez, have destroyed the richest country in the world, surely you wonder, what is my vision of the future for Venezuela.

Previously, I he pointed out that to some extent, the opposition has its share of responsibility for not creating a real feasibility project for the reconstruction of the country. The problem is not just to get out of chavismo, but the big problem is to know how to take on the authentic task of rebuilding the country.

If one day the regime falls, nobody believes, that in a year, or three, the country will rise from the ashes. And before this obvious fact, the opposition has to know how to face that reality.

There are those who have done studies, and believe that for Venezuela to return to the economic levels of 1975, they would have to spend 20 years of reconstruction. I, I am of the opinion, that if things are done well, in 5 or 6 years, the country could start to be prosperous. And for that, you do not have to wait for the oil barrel to reach 150 dollars. I insist, Germany, or Japan, countries that were totally destroyed in 1945 after World War II, in 5 years, they were already countries with stable economies, and they got it without having reserves of gold, or petroleum.

Many countries throughout history have gone through situations similar to that of Venezuela. Hitler, in Germany, was in power, and led the country to a tragedy, with a war, that destroyed the country. The Germans assumed after the defeat, that they had to dismantle the ideological infrastructures left by the Nazis (to de-Nazify Germany), and already in 1949, that country was heading to be the economic engine of Europe. But everything, it was not free. International aid led by the US, with the famous Marshall Plan in Europe, contributed to the strengthening of democracy in Western Europe. Another detail is that in Germany, the Nazi criminals were tried, and in Venezuela, something similar would have to happen. That is to say, the Chavismo culprits have to be judged and punished for their crimes. Moreover, I propose that instead of serving sentences in Venezuelan prisons, their sentences are met in Brazilian prisons, or in Argentine prisons.

After a hypothetical fall of the Chavista regime, the country will need its particular Marshall plan, where the international community has to contribute its bit, so that never again, a pseudo-communist populist, will return to power. Undoubtedly, I believe that MERCOSUR, or the OAS itself, could help in the reconstruction project of the country with a Marshall plan version.

Everything that I have commented previously, for some, possibly, will sound Chinese, or I would see it as very fanciful. But there are examples like those of Japan, or Germany, and Venezuela, unlike those countries, has a great advantage, since it still has human and natural resources to consolidate a possible reconstruction. If Marcos Pérez Jiménez, who governed Venezuela in five years (1953 1958), built a whole country with the most modern infrastructures for his time, I imagine that in the 21st century, another president, with some intelligence, could far exceed the works of Pérez Jiménez. In short, the country needs a group of leaders who know how to manage money and resources. I always say that if Japan had only 5% of the resources still left to Venezuela today, that Asian country would be the strongest economic power in the world.

I am of the idea that the Chavismo in the country must be eradicated from the root (Deschaveznificar). And one way is to outlaw the with chavista ideology, to judge those who support or glorify the figure of Chavez or Maduro, and to educate the new generations about the crimes committed in the name of the Bolivarian revolution.

I, from the beginning of 2001, maintain the thesis that if one day, a non-Chavista president comes to power in Venezuela, and the Chavistas are the main opposition party, that president, would not last 3 months in office. Can you imagine Nicolás Maduro, or Diosdado Cabello, as leaders of the opposition, and their followers forming barricades in the streets glorifying the revolution? That is the dramatic reality that we would find, if the Chavistas are allowed to remain loose there.

So, I am very clear, that for the country to go one day ahead, the first thing that needs to be done is to eradicate the chavismo from the institutions, and from the life of the country. In short, deschaveznificar Venezuela.

By the way, those who would have to assume that role, that of extirpating chavism, would have to be the international community, as they did in Germany in 1945, after the defeat of the Nazis with the Nuremberg trials. That is to say, the international community would be in charge of investigating the crimes committed by Chavism, creating a kind of International Criminal Court to judge Chavistas hierarchs. Those crimes to judge would go from cases of corruption, political persecution, assassinations, to what I would call selective genocide.

I insist, if Venezuela's chavism is not removed, I doubt, that the country can return to a path of prosperity. Undoubtedly, the investors, the companies that left the country, the thousands and thousands of Venezuelans (lawyers, engineers, doctors, architects, etc.) would not risk returning to a country with chavista leaders lurking to take power again. I insist ... the Chavistas, they have to be eradicated from society, as in their day, they were the Nazis in Germany, or the Communists in Eastern Europe.

I am not the only one with the idea, that the international

community judges the Chavistas. For example, last August of 2018, a group of six countries, made up of Argentina, Canada, Chile, Colombia, Paraguay, and Peru, decided to file a joint complaint with the International Criminal Court (ICC) Prosecutor to investigate the commission of crimes of lese humanity in Venezuela by the Maduro regime. And if we add to that the detail, that in that Court there are more than 600 registered cases of crimes against humanity in Venezuela, I believe, that the denunciation of the governments of six countries, could influence that to some extent, that the rest of the democratic world, join the denunciation, so that Maduro, and his accomplices, one day, be tried outside of Venezuela. In fact, in mid-October 2018, Costa Rica joined the list, and it was expected that more countries add be targeted, such as France and Germany.

But not everything is optimistic that one day, we can see a trial of Maduro sitting in the Court of The Hague. There is already a precedent with another dictator, the president of Sudan, Omar Al Bashir, who has two arrest warrants issued against him by the ICC in 2009 and 2010, and in 2018, he continued to rule in his country, as if nothing happened.

The issue is that in the case of Venezuela, unlike that of Sudan, there is more evidence and facts, which could create a precedent in the world. There are many reports issued by a diversity of international organizations, which show that in Venezuela, human rights are violated every day.

For example, in February 2018, the OAS published a report in which it collected more than 12,000 cases of arbitrary detention since 2015, and more than 8,000 extrajudicial executions. In said document, it is stated that there was "sufficient basis" to consider that the Venezuelan government had committed crimes against humanity.

In the complaint lodged before the Court of The Hague by the six heads of government, it is important to highlight that they have included two reports prepared by international experts, which document extrajudicial processes, torture and arbitrary detentions.

In short, I hope that to some extent, the ICC of The Hague, is to some extent, the Nuremberg of the Chavistas. And in case of finding guilty, that they fully comply with their sentences in Brazilian prisons, or Colombian prisons. Never on Venezuelan soil.

IS THE PRESIDENT LEGALLY MADURO?

In this chapter, I want to make a brief summary of the entire story I have released throughout the book. If anyone still has doubts about the legality of Maduro as president, with the following, for sure, I clarify those doubts.

After the death of Hugo Chávez in 2013, Maduro had been designated as the successor, by finger, by his political father (Chávez), skipping, or violating, the Chavez constitution, when, who should have assumed the position, was the president of parliament, the ultra chavista Diosdado Cabello. All the opposition, and the international community, criticized, complained, threatened. And in the end, Maduro, assumed illegally, the country's presidency.

When Maduro convened the Constituent Assembly, everyone, nationally, and internationally, condemned and did not recognize that Constituent, because the Chavist constitution was violated, by not clearly fulfilling the norms for its convocation. That is, everyone shouted to heaven, and Maduro, continued as if nothing.

Later, that "illegal" Constituent Assembly convened presidential elections for 2018, and initially, the opposition was encouraged to participate in those elections. Later, the opposition manifested, that this convocation was illegal, since it did not comply with the constitutional norm. In short, ... it is more than evident that an illegally created a Constituent, that calls for a presidential election, its decisions, can not be taken as of character legal.

And after the expected victory of Maduro in May 2018, returns again the protests both nationally and internationally, condemning that Maduro, won a manipulated election. The

OAS, governments of different countries, foreign leaders, unanimously agreed that Maduro was a usurper in the presidency of Venezuela.

From May 2018, to January 10, 2019, in all that time, the opposition, and the international community, crossed their arms, waiting for Maduro's takeover of power before the Supreme Court of Justice chavista in Venezuela.

For almost a year, everyone knew, that this Maduro would illegally assume the presidency of Venezuela, since he would have to have assumed the position before the National Assembly (formed by the opposition majority). Once again, all the opposition, and the international community, condemn, but they do nothing concrete.

On January 23, Juan Guaidó, in a somewhat atypical way, proclaimed himself provisional president.

But Guaidó does not have full powers, and now, everyone expects, that the leadership of the corrupt military high command that exists in Venezuela, one day, decide to stop supporting Maduro, which, I think, would never happen, because that Venezuelan military high, is rotten in corruption that has created Chavismo in more than 20 years, in order to remain in power.

As in Cuba, communism has been in power for more than 60 years in the island thanks in large part to corruption within the armed forces in that country. In fact, the Chavista model is an improved copy of Castro's model. Undoubtedly, Maduro has surpassed his teacher Hugo Chávez, and Chávez's teacher, Fidel Castro.

AND WHAT HAVE I DONE FOR
MY COUNTRY?

And if you ask yourself, what have I done for my country ...

Well, as I mentioned at the beginning of the book, as a child, I had identified very much with the world of politics, and I thought at the time, that the ideology that represented the Christian Democratic Party COPEI, was the most just for my country. When I turned 18, I joined the national secretariat of youth organization of the party, and actively participated in various electoral campaigns, supporting the candidates, and an ideology, which brought stability and prosperity to the country.

In the 80s, and beginning of the 90s, I worked in the Supreme Electoral Council, helping in some way in the consolidation of democracy. I lived the first elections of mayors and governors in Venezuela, where I participated with great enthusiasm. One of my fondest memories, was to work as a coordinator of a polling station, despite, that two days before the elections, I suffered an accident that had left me in an unsuitable condition to leave home. In fact, they had gone to look for me at my house, and between two people, they helped me move to the voting center. I was on crutches, and despite the pain and discomfort, I felt happy to contribute to my country.

In 1993, after the expulsion of the founder of COPEI, Rafel Caldera, I left the party, and went to be part of what would be known as Convergencia, a new group, which brought together several parties in support of Caldera, and that he contributed greatly to being elected president in 1993.

At the end of the 80s, I started writing opinion articles, for different newspapers that were published in Venezuela, highlighting among them, the newspaper El Universal, where I was a columnist writer.

I remember the day of the fall of the Berlin Wall, with the demise of communist regimes in Eastern Europe, and the hope that democracy would come to Cuba.

The question is that while some countries were liberated from tyranny, others, 10 years later, like Nicaragua, El Salvador, Bolivia, would appear the old ghosts that had been overcome would , and this time, the weapons and money, They would not come directly from Cuba. Now would come from from the Chavez regime in Venezuela.

As I mentioned at the beginning of the book, I had to experience the tragic events of the "Caracazo" in 1993, and the two military coup attempts of 1994. I lived in the first person as a part of Venezuelan society, renegade from his past, looking for the image of a military coup, the solution to problems.

In the face of the evident triumph of Hugo Chávez in an election, in 1996 I decided to leave my job, house and family, and go to the land of my ancestors, Spain. Unwittingly, I had become an exiled.

Sometimes, I say that the world goes around so many times. My maternal grandparents, in 1935, left Spain, escaping from communism, hiding in a ship, which supposedly went to Argentina. That ship, arrived in a country called Venezuela, and there, they were welcomed without a coin in their pockets. With work, and sacrifice, they were able to move forward, in a country that knew how to welcome thousands of people who escaped many conflicts, such as the Second World War. 60 years later, who would say that history would have the whim to change things. Now, those grandchildren of Spaniards, who like me, have been born in Venezuela, have decided to pack their bags, and escape the same danger that in some measure forced their grandparents to leave their country of origin.

Fernando Germán M

After the triumph of Chávez in 1998, a group of Venezuelans in Madrid, we organized, to denounce before Spanish society, the abuses of the new regime. So I participated in the organization of some demonstrations in La Puerta del Sol, in El Retiro Park in Madrid, or in front of the Venezuelan embassy.

In the year 2000, I participated in the creation, together with a group of Venezuelans, of the Democratic Platform of Venezuelans in Spain, whose main role was to denounce the rise of the dictatorship in Venezuela.

Later, at the beginning of 2004, in Madrid, I worked as an editor and journalist in a magazine, dedicated to highlighting the integration of the Venezuelan community residing in Spain.

After some discussions and disagreements with members of the Democratic Platform, I decided to move away, and later, at the end of that year 2004, I moved out of Madrid.

In that year, I had to see, as in the Venezuelan community itself, there were some conflicts within the opposition to the regime. Moreover, there were two democratic platforms, each of which went its own way, and in some cases, some of its members were more radical than the Chavistas themselves. In this atmosphere of confrontation, which was a reflection of what was lived in Venezuela, began to emerge the so-called "ni nis", who were people they did not like so much with the Chavistas, and the opponents.

After getting married, I decided to leave political activity, and dedicate myself to my family and my work.

After the last events in Venezuela and in Spain in 2018, I thought, it is time to resume the activity, and that is why I have decided to write this book, as a small contribution to the reconstruction of the country.

I am Venezuelan, and I believe that one day, my country will wake up and be able to move forward. Several countries that lived bloody civil wars because of communism, today are emerging powers, with democracies as stable models.

I hope, with this book, to some extent, contribute to many people understand, that with the so-called "populism", problems are not solved, if not, that does the opposite. Venezuela, or Nicaragua, are a clear example of this, and I think it is ridiculous, that people outside this reality, defend a model of dictatorial regime.

MY FINAL WISH

And to finish my book, I just want to say, that I wish, that one day not very far, I can return to my free land of the populist Chavista communist dictatorship, and be able to see and embrace my mother, brothers, nephews, cousins, friends, whom for years, I do not see them in person, because of the regime.

Aspiro, that after the fall of the dictatorship, I can participate, as far as possible, in this important task of rebuilding a free and democratic Venezuela.

I insist … rebuilding a whole country is not an easy task. I insist, if things are done well, applying only logic, and knowing how to manage and dispose of resources, the country can emerge with everyone's effort.

I hope, that in about 5 years, my family and friends, me digan "Fernando, you were right" about the reality of the reconstruction of the country.

But if the international community (OAS, MERCOSUR, UN, G7, EU, etc.), continue giving nice speeches, and do not move a single finger to end the dictatorship in Venezuela, we will have Chavismo for about 50 more years, and that great desire of reconstruction of the country, would only be in dead letters in an old book.

I insist, without a clear intervention action by the international community, I see a solution in the Venezuelan case very difficult.

It is not enough for the OAS, the EU, or 120 countries to recognize Guaidó as interim president of Venezuela. Maduro does not care, and laughs at it.

By the way, to give you a funny idea of that bloody reality in Venezuela, then I reproduce a caricature, where the Cuban dictator Raul Castro appears. Such a caricature could be valid for other characters, such as Russian President Vladimir Putin or Turkish Erdoğan.

I hope that in about 6, or 8 years, I can write another book, where I count, how Venezuela, was able to overcome the worst crisis in its history.

Now they are, 10:15 in the afternoon (Venezuelan time), May 23, 2019.

www.ingramcontent.com/pod-product-compliance
Lightning Source LLC
Chambersburg PA
CBHW010721110626
46523CB00046B/693